EGYPTIAN LEGENDS
and Stories

Frontispiece: Maat, the Goddess of Truth

EGYPTIAN LEGENDS

and Stories

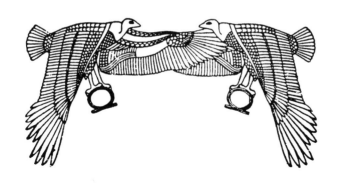

M.V. SETON-WILLIAMS

The Rubicon Press
57 Cornwall Gardens
London SW7 4BE

First published 1988
Reprinted 1990
Reprinted 1995
Reprinted 1998

British Library Cataloguing-in-Publication Data.

A catalogue record for this book is available from the British Library.

ISBN 0-948695-08-0

Designed and typeset by The Rubicon Press

Printed and bound in Great Britain by
Biddles Limited of Guildford and King's Lynn

CONTENTS

To Margaret Murray

ACKNOWLEDGEMENTS

My purpose in writing *Egyptian Legends and Stories* is to satisfy the many requests I have received for them over the past twenty-five years from passengers I have lectured to on the Nile Cruises.

As a child I read 'The Prince and the Three Fates', published by Andrew Lang in *The Brown Fairy Book*, and since then I have collected many more. Some of these were originally included in Margaret Murray's book, *Ancient Egyptian Legends*, which is long since out of print.

I particularly wish to thank Miss M.O. Millar for a number of the original drawings, and Mrs. Angela Godfrey for the others, maps and for typing my manuscript, together with Mrs. Gene Bridgeman. To Jonathan Cape Ltd. for permission to reproduce part of George Sefaris's poem 'Helen', and Kodensha for the colour slide from my book *Les Tresors de Toutankhamon*. The table of dates follows that in the *Introduction to Ancient Egypt* by T.G.H. James and I thank him for his permission to use it. I would also like to thank my publishers, The Rubicon Press.

INTRODUCTION

From ancient times the land of Egypt has been a source of all kinds of literature: hymns, songs, poems, prayers, plays, stories and maxims. These were recorded by scribes and priests and are some of the earliest stories we know of. The Egyptians believed in an ordered way of life exemplified by the Goddess Maat, the Goddess of Truth, Justice and Moral Integrity. They were also a very religious people and the majority of their stories are based on religious themes, with good triumphing over evil. They had Wisdom Texts similar to, but far earlier than the Book of Proverbs. One from the Old Kingdom, 'The Instructions of Ptah-hotep' reads:

"Be not arrogant because of your knowledge, and have no confidence because you are learned. Take counsel with the ignorant as well as the wise, for the limits of knowledge cannot be reached, and no one really knows the end. Good words are more precious than malachite, and yet they can be found with slave-girls at the millstones."

The life of a scribe was described as being ideal and the schoolboy was advised to follow that instead of being a farmer or a soldier. There is one maxim that strongly advises against a farmer's life:

"I am told that you have foresaken writing and given yourself up to pleasure. You have set your mind on work in the fields and have turned your back on the words of God. Think what happens to the farmer when the harvest is registered (for taxation purposes). The insects have eaten half the grain, and the hippopotamus has eaten the rest. The mice are eating up what remains, and there is a horde of locusts. There are plenty of sparrows and pigeons eating what is left. Woe to the farmer . . . The scribe, however, directs the work. For him there are no taxes, he pays his tribute in writing. How good to be a scribe."

1

The object in producing this collection of Egyptian stories and legends is to present some of the earliest tales in a form more easily understood, and to include some favourite ones from medieval times. So now enjoy your stories which should all start, "A long time ago . . .

DATES OF RELEVANT DYNASTIES

ARCHAIC

First Dynasty	c. 3100-2890 B.C.
Second Dynasty	c. 2890-2686 B.C.

OLD KINGDOM

Third Dynasty	c. 2686-2613 B.C.
Fourth Dynasty	c. 2613-2494 B.C.
Fifth Dynasty	c. 2494-2345 B.C.
Sixth Dynasty	c. 2345-2181 B.C.

MIDDLE KINGDOM

Eleventh Dynasty	c. 2133-1991 B.C.
Twelfth Dynasty	c. 1991-1786 B.C.

NEW KINGDOM

Eighteenth Dynasty	c. 1567-1320 B.C.
Nineteenth Dynasty	c. 1320-1200 B.C.
Twentieth Dynasty	c. 1200-1085 B.C.

THE GODS OF WRITING

The deities that were particularly associated with writing were Sheshat, Sefkhet-Abwy and Thoth. Sheshat, who was the earliest goddess shown in this connection dates from the Second Dynasty onwards. She is portrayed as a woman wearing a plain dress covered by a long panther-skin robe with the tail hanging down to her feet. Her emblem appears as a star or rosette standing up from her headband, or possibly, a frond of papyrus tucked into it.

Sheshat held pride of place and recorded not only the king's jubilees and the cattle count, but also the king's campaigns. When she is pictured listing the king's regnal years she holds a notched palm branch terminating in a tadpole, the ritual sign for one hundred thousand years, which in turn is set on the sign for eternity. She also acted as librarian and supervised the establishment of the temple libraries.

The other goddess of writing, Sefkhet-Abwy, does not appear until the Eighteenth Dynasty and may well be another form of Sheshat. She is shown as a woman with a seven pointed star on her head, usually under an inverted bow. Among her functions was the encouragement of writing and attending the foundation ceremony of "Stretching the Cord", when the king with her help measured the ground plan of the temples before they were constructed. She also appears in her role of recorder, writing the king's name on the leaves of the sacred tree, the Ished tree.

Thoth was the vizier of the gods, presiding over scribes and learning. He was also the God of Wisdom. As one of the moon gods, he was regarded as the reckoner of time (the Egyptians used a lunar month). He wears on his head the crescent moon and disc. He was also considered to be the scribe of the Goddess Maat and of Re and was often shown carrying the writing reed and palette

3

Sheshat   Sefkhet-Abwy

of the scribe. The principal seat of the worship of Thoth was el-
Ashmunein, Hermopolis (ancient Khemennu) in Middle Egypt,
where Re was supposed to have rested after creating the world. At
Hermopolis, Thoth was head of an Ennead of eight gods who were
primordial deities.

The name of Thoth seems to have been derived from *tehu*, an
early name of the ibis, and Thoth is shown associated with this
bird from the Late Predynastic Period onwards. He is usually depicted with the head of an ibis. He is also connected with the
baboon *(Papio cynocephalus)*, probably from the First Dynasty
onwards. The baboon is always shown squatting on a plinth or
with arms raised in worship of the sun. Thoth appears in the Judgement scene where he records the weight of the deceased's heart

4

Thoth (as ibis)   *Thoth (as baboon)*

and his deeds. He is also known as "Lord of the Sacred Words" and the mediator and the messenger of the gods. This led to him being identified in the Ptolemaic Period as Hermes and as the "Twice Great" or "Trismegistos" of the classical writers. In certain texts Thoth is regarded as being either self-created or created from the heart of Re, with whom he is always closely associated.

A hymn to Thoth on one of the columns of the hall at Philae says in part "Thou art the god who is high on his standard, who came forth from the god himself (Re); for whom opened the doors of the eastern horizon of Re by whom he was begotten. Every god came forth at his command - what he spoke was accomplished. You are the god who prot.cted Horus, with the Eye (of Re) do you also protect King Ptolemy. For you are Thoth . . ."

THE CREATION OF THE WORLD

The Ancient Egyptians had many creator gods. Thus the world or more specifically Egypt was created in diverse ways in various parts of the country. What follows is a short selection of the better known myths of the creation.

1 THE CREATION ACCORDING TO HELIOPOLIS

This is based on British Museum Papyrus 10188, version B.

In the beginning there was nothing but the watery waste of Nun. There was no light, there was no darkness, there was nothing solid to rest upon. Then in the watery waste of Nun something stirred. It was the god Atum, in his form of Khepre the "Becoming One" who was the rising sun. At first he had nothing to rest upon so he made a solid bank. The Egyptians imagined this to be a muddy island rising out of the watery waste, which resembled the Nile Flood when it was going down leaving small islands in its wake.

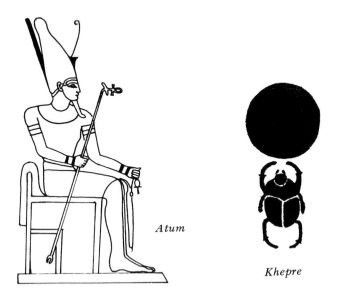

Atum

Khepre

Atum realised that he had a great deal to do, so he created two other gods to help him. These were Shu and Tefnut, the God of the Air and the Goddess of Moisture. They were nearly always represented in human form. Shu was represented as a man with a feather on his head and Tefnut though a woman, also shown as a lioness. They were identified with Menhit at Latopolis (Esna), and Nehemauit at Hermopolis (al-Ashmunein). Tefnut was the Goddess of Rain, Dew and the Gentle Winds, not to be confused with the fierce ones that blew in from the desert. Shu and Tefnut were universal Egyptian gods and do not appear to have had any special shrines or places connected with them.

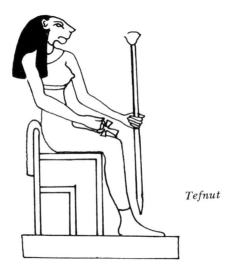

Tefnut

After they had been created, they in turn produced Geb, the Earth God, and Nut, the Sky Goddess. Geb is usually shown as a man wearing either the White Crown or the Atef Crown, or a goose, the bird sacred to him, and whose name is a play upon his. The earth was called the "House of Geb". Again Geb had no particular shrine but was worshipped throughout Egypt though he may have had special connections with Edfu and Dendera, which was known as "the home of the Children of Geb". Both Nut and Geb have strong connections with the Afterworld. Nut, the Sky Goddess was originally only the goddess of the day sky resting upon the mountains of Baki and Manu (the farther mountains of dawn and dusk), but by the Late Period, she represented the sky both by day and by night. The goddess is usually depicted as a woman bearing on her head a vase of water, the hieroglyph with the phonetic value of Nut. Sometimes she is shown as a woman with horns and a disc, usually worn by the goddess Hathor. But more commonly she is shown as a woman or a cow spangled with stars, arched over the body of her husband Geb, or sometimes supported by her father Shu. The sun was thought to have been swallowed by Nut, passing through her body to be reborn every day. This

Shu, Geb and Nut

scene is shown in several tombs, and in the Chapel of the New Year at Dendera. Nut was always regarded as friend and protector of the dead. She is frequently referred to as mother Nut, and is supposed to spread herself out over the dead in her name of "Coverer of the Sky". She was expected to supply the dead with food and drink, but because she was also their protector, is often portrayed on the inner side of coffin lids, where she could closely supervise what was happening to the dead person.

Nut had her own sacred tree, the sycamore, situated at Heliopolis and she is sometimes shown as a woman coming forth from a tree. The branches of this tree became a refuge for weary souls resting from the heat of the midday sun, where they could be refreshed by the food on which the goddess also lived. This sycamore was the archetype of the traditional tree under which the Holy Family rested on their flight to Egypt. The skeleton of the last of these sycamores is still to be seen today at Matariah, a suburb of Heliopolis.

Geb and Nut had five children born on the five epagnol days of the year. The story goes that Re cursed Nut, and that according to this curse her children were not to be born on any one day of the year. The ancient Egyptians had a lunar calendar of 360 days, so that the year was always getting out of order. This story accounts for the addition of five days to the traditional year. Thoth, the Moon God and Reckoner of Time, played dice with the official Moon God, Aah, a shadowy being figuring little in Egyptian mythology, and won from him the light of five whole nights, and with his help was able to create five whole days on which the children of Nut were born. These days lay outside the official year so that the curse of Re had no effect, because they were over the official year. Osiris was born on the first day, Horus the Elder on the second day, Seth on the third day, Isis on the fourth day and Nephthys on the fifth day.

Osiris was represented as a mummified man standing upright or seated upon his throne all in white. He wore the Atef Crown (represented by the horizontal horns of *Ovis longipes,* surmounted by a disc and two plumes) and held the crook and flail that were to become the royal emblems.

Horus the Elder was one of the great leader gods of Egypt. He is shown as a man or as a man with the head of a hawk or falcon, sometimes with a sun disc upon his head. He was a sky god and a sun god, and his cult was one of the most ancient in Egypt, going back at least to predynastic times. There are many forms of Horus, but gradually Horus, Hor or Heru absorbed them all. The sun was the right eye of Horus, and the moon the left eye. For moonless nights, a form of the Eyeless Horus was worshipped in the Western Delta. The original home of Horus was in this Western

Delta, in the Third Nome, or district of Lower Egypt, at Temait-en-Hor, now Damanhur (the town of Horus). From the beginning he was closely associated with a tree and cow goddess, a form of Hathor, whose name means "House of Horus", and who was originally regarded as his nurse. Naturally as time went on he became confused with Horus, the son of Osiris and Isis, though originally they were completely distinct. The four children of Horus were demi-gods whose job it was to guard the canopic jars in which the viscera of the dead were placed. They are usually shown as four small mummified figures, each with a different head - those of a hawk, a man, a jackal and an ape. Horus the Elder's place of worship was transferred to Upper Egypt after the conquest of the North by the South and centred on Edfu, where Horus the Behdt was worshipped. He was a form of Horus the Elder, the harpooner, but again he became hopelessly confused with his counterpart.

Seth was a very old deity. His early attributes were very different from his later ones. Originally he was closely associated with Horus and appeared as a friend and helper of the dead. He was initially one of the two gods pouring purified water over the king, but in later scenes he is replaced by Thoth. The significance of the name of Seth is not easy to determine, nor can the animal associated with him be satisfactorily identified. He is a desert god and associated with the night and all dark and frightening things; the opposite in fact of Horus the Sky God. Later he fights with the Younger Horus for the control of Egypt, and is defeated and killed in the form of a great red hippopotamus, as depicted on the walls of the temple at Edfu. A miracle play depicting this event used to be enacted annually on the Sacred Lake at Edfu.

The next to be born was Isis, the Mistress of Magic. She was the sister and wife of Osiris, and mother of the Younger Horus. There is a remarkable Greek inscription which was discovered on two identical texts, one on the island of Ios and the other on the island of Andros, which describes the attributes of Isis. It reads in part:

> I am Isis, the Mistress of Every Land
> I was taught by Hermes (Thoth) and by his help
>   I found out demotic script,

that all things should not be written with the
   same letter
I laid down laws for mankind, and I ordained things
   which no one has the power to change
   (like the goddess Sheshet)
I am the eldest daughter of Kronos (Geb)
I am the wife and sister of Osiris the King
I am she who governs Sothis
I am she who is called divine among Egyptian women
Foɪ me was built the city of Bubastis
I divided the earth from the sky
I marked out the path of the stars
I prescribed the course of the sun and the moon . . .
   (Inscriptionses Graecae, Vol. XII, fasc. V, pt. l)

The last to be born was Nephthys (or Nebt-Het), who like Isis
was a goddess of the dead and the sister and wife of Seth. Her
name means "Lady of the House" (the house in this case being the
sky). She is shown as a woman, or as a kite when mourning Osiris.
Her position as protector of the dead seems to have been more important than her position vis-à-vis Seth, and she must originally
have been an independent goddess. She is always shown in human
form with her symbol (her hieroglyph) on her head, which repres-
ents her name. With Isis she stands behind Osiris when the hearts
of the dead are weighed. With Isis she laments Osiris. And like Isis
she has many forms.

2   THE MEMPHITE THEOLOGY

When the First Dynasty established its capital at Memphis just to the south of the present position of Cairo at the junction of Upper and Lower Egypt, it was felt necessary for the priesthood to claim precedence for their creator god Ptah. This, unlike the other Egyptian creations, was not a physical but an intellectual creation by the Word and the Mind of God. The text describing this is written on the Shabaka Stone No. 498 in the British Museum. The present text dates to the eighth century B.C. to the reign of Shabaka of the Twenty-fifth Dynasty, who reigned from c. 716-702 B.C. However, it is a copy of a much older document. It has been published various times, one of the more recent translations being by Pritchard *(Ancient Near Eastern Texts, 5)*. It is the most advanced of all the Egyptian Creation texts. Unfortunately at some later date the basalt block on which it was inscribed was used as a grindstone, making a difficult text even more complicated to decipher.

The inscription begins with a reference to the struggle between Horus and Seth for the possession of Egypt, recording that the struggle finally ceased in the "Balance of the Two Lands" which is the name of the temple of Ptah at Memphis. The various forms of Ptah are then listed: Father of Fathers, Mother of Mothers as in the case of Neith-Ptah - the Heart and Tongue of the Ennead, Ptah who gave birth to all other gods. Ptah formed the tongue and the heart which were in the form of Atum. But the greatest of these is Ptah who gave life to all the gods as well as to their *Kas*, through the heart by which Horus became Ptah, and through the tongue by which Thoth became Ptah. So it was that the heart and tongue gained control over every other part of the body, by teaching that Ptah is in everything, in every body, in every mouth of all the gods, and in all men, all cattle, all fish, in every creeping thing, and everything that lives. What he thinks, he commands and thus everything he wishes comes to pass. His Ennead, which are the gods associated with him at Memphis, were created by his tongue, which pronounced the name of everything from which all the gods came, when their names were said with Shu and Tefnut. Everything was formed when their names were pronounced: the sight, the hearing and the breathing were all contrived by the heart. It is the heart which conceived everything and the tongue which gave it utterance. Thus it was that all the gods were formed and Ptah's Ennead completed, all coming from what the heart thought and the tongue spoke.

Thus it was said of Ptah that he created everything and brought all the gods into being. Thus he is indeed Ta-tenen (the Earth-god form of Ptah) who brought forth the gods because everything came forth from him (that is the earth), all food and drink, the gods' offerings, and every other good thing. So after the creation Ptah was satisfied, because he had created everything including the Divine Order. He had formed the gods, he had built the

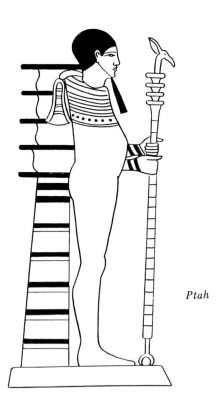

Ptah

cities, he had divided Egypt into districts, he had placed the gods in their shrines, set up their figures and supplied their offerings. Then the gods entered into their bodies in whatever material they were formed, of wood, stone, clay or metal or of any other material that might grow upon the earth. As a result the gods were satisfied with the work of Ptah.

Ptah was the God of Craftsmen and is always represented as a mummified man standing in a shrine holding a staff in his hand with an amulet round his neck.

This philosophical conception of the creation was the most advanced that the Egyptian priesthood conceived. It had broad concepts not realised by the other cults. It imagined Ptah as the mind of the Universe, whose thoughts and words produced everything in heaven and earth, the other gods merely being forms of his thoughts. In that way he could truly claim to be the eternal single god alone in the Universe. Light came from him, and by his breath of life every living thing had its existence. The difficulty is that we do not know when this concept was first formulated. It certainly goes back several millennia, but it is not known how early. There is nothing as advanced as this concept until the New Testament. The same idea is conveyed in many of the hymns to Ptah, where Ptah is seen as having derived his power from Ptah-Tatenen (the text of which is produced by Lepsius in *Denkmaler* VI). This probably dates to the latter part of the second millennium B.C. "O Hidden One whose eternal form is unknown, Lord of the Years, giver of life at will".

3   THE CREATION ACCORDING TO HERMOPOLIS

The other great school of religious thought after Heliopolis was Hermopolis in Middle Egypt. Here eight gods and goddesses were worshipped. Nu and Nunet, Amun and Amunet, Heh and Hehut, Ke and Kekut. These eight gods were known as the Ogdoad of Hermopolis and were regarded by some as the oldest gods in Egypt. The original mound from which the land of Egypt developed was supposed to have appeared at Hermopolis. It was here that the Sun God was supposed to have taken his stand having been created by the eight gods. It will be seen later this was not the only creation that the Sun God was supposed to have had.

Nu and Nunet stood for the primeval abyss out of which the world was created, while Amun and Amunet stood for the Hidden Ones. The others stood for mist and darkness. They were in fact the eight primeval deities from which everything developed. Associated with them was Thoth, the God of Wisdom, called in Egyptian, Djhuti, and in Greek, Hermes. He is a moon god, a reckoner of time, and the Vizier of the Gods. Depicted as an ibis-headed man, his sacred animals are the baboon and the ibis, but this is really because there is a play upon their names in Egyptian. Thoth was thought to have invented writing, and wrote a book in which all the wisdom of the world was entered. One of his tasks was the restoration of the Eye of Re, after it had been stolen by Seth. Hermopolis was known as the City of the Eight, and was a double city. The gods in this group of eight were all frog-headed and the goddesses all serpent-headed. Copies of the Book of Thoth existed in the temples and it was to this that the Greeks referred when they spoke of the Hermetic Books of the Egyptians. In the Judgement scene, it is Thoth who checks the scales, and Thoth who writes down the judgement. He was both the scribe of the Gods and the Vizier acting for Re during his absence, taking over also from Osiris in certain cases. He was also known as the "Twice Great".

16

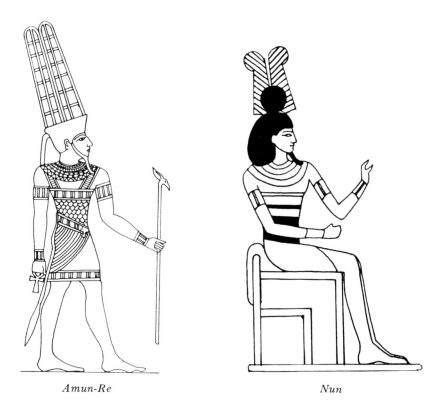

Amun-Re   Nun

There is no creation story of Thoth or of the other gods of Hermopolis, except that it was claimed that the primeval hill from which the whole land came, first appeared here, and that here Re took his stand upon it. Undoubtedly there were disputes between the priesthood of Hermopolis and that of Heliopolis, who had anyway a far more developed story. At some point the priests of Heliopolis gained the mastery, for the temple services carried on throughout Egypt were based on that of Heliopolis.

4   THE CREATION ACCORDING TO EDFU (BEHEDET)

This account comes from the texts upon the walls of the temple at Edfu.

In the beginning there was the watery waste of Nun. When this subsided as did the annual flood, it left a sandy island. On this island was a perch, and here a falcon, which represented Horus, rested. However, he had an enemy in the form of a snake, and he had to have a protector, in fact two protector gods to prevent him being attacked. These gods also protected Horus with the "Great White One", the ceremonial stone macehead with which Egyptian kings are shown killing their enemies. Horus, "he of the dappled plumage" - for here one is dealing with the elder hawk god, the brother of Osiris - sweeps in from the sky and takes his place in the earliest temple. This was at first made of reeds, and consisted of an enclosure with a small sacred part at one end where the emblems of the gods were kept. As time went on this temple became enlarged, first built of brick and later in its final stages of stone. Horus, whose name Har means the "Distant One", planes through the sky, which is his home, on his powerful wings.

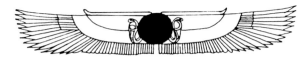

Winged disc

He is closely linked with Re and the other sun gods and his home is with Hathor, whose name Hat-Hor means "House of Horus", and who is another very old sky and cow goddess. At the end of Egyptian history, the various forms of Horus become indistinguishable, and Horus the Elder becomes one with Horus the Younger, the son of Osiris.

18

Horus the Elder

The Egyptians envisaged not only the creation of the world, but the end of the world, as described in Chapter 175 of the *Book of the Dead* thus: "This earth will return to the Primeval Water Nun, to the endless flood as it was in the beginning. And in the end there will be no gods and no goddesses. Nothing but Atum the Lord of All who made all mankind and all the gods, and who exists when everything else passes away." Then Atum and Osiris will have become one.

5   THE CREATION ACCORDING TO SAIS - ESNA

One of the fullest accounts of the creation is that from Esna (Serge Sauneron, Les Fêtes Religieuses d'Esna, *Esna* V, p. 273) found in the temple of Khnum dating to the second century A.D. This is obviously based on a very much earlier text originating in Sais, and attributes the creation and that of Re to Neith the Archer Goddess of Sais. Neith is a very old Delta goddess always represented as a woman with a bow and crossed arrows on her head or in her hands, and usually wearing the Red Crown of Lower Egypt.

It begins with the creation of Neith that took place before the creation of the world. When there was no land, no vegetation, nothing except the watery waste of Nun, Neith too changes her aspect; she becomes in turn a great *Lates* fish and a cow, but what matters is not what form she takes, but that she has come into existence as a form with a conscience in this vast formless void. Once she has begun to think, creation as she imagines it proceeds at once. Her first creation is Egypt, which emerges as she says in gladness. After this she creates the thirty gods by pronouncing their names. They greet her and are grateful that she has given them something to rest upon, and that she has separated night from day for them. Neith tells the gods to lift themselves onto the earth to escape from the great lassitude that is engendered by the watery waste.

The gods are worried about what will happen next, and who else is to be created. Neith takes the form of a cow and begins to meditate on what she will create next. She speaks and tells the gods that an all-powerful god will be born on that day. When He opens his eyes light will come; when He closes his eyes darkness will fall. Men will be born from the tears of His eyes, and gods will be formed from the saliva of His lips. Neith promises that she will protect him and render him vigorous with her vigour. She foretells

Neith

that His children will rebel against him, but that they will be beaten in His name, as he is my son, and He will be king of this country forever. His name will be Khepre in the morning, Atum in the evening, and he will be known as Re forever and ever. When Re was born of Neith he was placed in an egg from which came the sacrosanct god Re. His mother Neith called him to come to her, and he opened his eyes and the sun shone, but because he could not see her at first, he wept and men were formed "of the tears of his eyes". Because there must always be a balance between good and evil, in the hour of the birth of Re, Apopi was born, a serpent 120 cubits long, in whose heart was rebellion against Re.

6 THE DESTRUCTION OF MANKIND BY RE

This legend comes from a side chapel in the Tomb of Sety I.

In the beginning mankind was grateful to Re for the benefits that he had conferred upon them, and they worshipped him and supplied all the things necessary for his service. After a while, however, they became tired of doing this and claimed that Re had grown old, and had no need of further offerings, so supplies for the temples diminished.

Re consulted with the Council of the Gods as to what he should do, but he did it secretly so that mankind should not know what he was about to do. The gods came together and grouped themselves around Re, and asked him what he wished to say. First he consulted the god Nun, because he was the God of the Watery Waste and older than the other gods. Nun advised him to send his Eye against mankind. Now his Eye was his daughter Sekhmet, sometimes known as Hathor. In her form of Sekhmet she was a fierce lioness fond of hunting, and stood for the fierce rays of the midday sun. She went forth and slew man in the valley and in the desert where they had taken refuge. Then Re was sorry for mankind and he called to the goddess to cease her work and come to him in peace, as mankind had been punished enough. But the lioness roared and said "I swore by my life that when I gained mastery over men it was very satisfying to my heart". Then again Re took council with the gods to see how he could stop Sekhmet's slaughter, as she was devouring mankind and wading in their blood.

The gods advised Re to give Sekhmet beer, of which she was very fond. So large quantities of beer were brewed and mixed with some Kharkady (red stain) so that it resembled blood. Then when the goddess was resting this was poured upon the fields where she

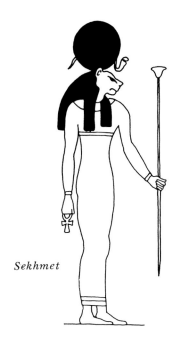

Sekhmet

was about to hunt next morning, and it reached the height of four spans. And His Majesty Re said "I will protect men with this beer which I have made." And when the goddess went out at daybreak she found all the ground flooded with liquid. She admired her face in the flood, and then she drank the beer and her heart became glad, and she did not know in what part of the land she was, and because she was drunk she fell asleep and mankind was saved. And the Majesty of this god said to Sekhmet "Come in peace." Ever since that time jars of soporific beer have been prepared at the festivals of Sekhmet-Hathor, and at Dendera there was a festival of Drunkeness.

The story of Osiris is to be found in Plutarch, *De Iside et Osiride*. This tale is mainly from the Margaret Murray version.

When Osiris was born there were many marvels and wonders, prodigies and signs. A voice was said to have been heard over all the earth saying "The Lord of All comes forward to the light." A woman drawing water from one of the sacred wells rushed out saying "Osiris the King is born."

Now traditionally at the time of the birth of Osiris, Egypt was a barbarous country where men were constantly at war, and where cannibalism was practised. Osiris became the king of a small state in the Delta, Busiris, and from there he moved to become king of all Egypt. He taught his people to cultivate the land and to

Osiris

plant grain, wheat and barley, to grow vines, to make laws and to abolish their savage customs. This he continued to do for many years, until having subdued the Egyptians he went on to give the arts of civilization to Western Asia.

His brother Seth hated Osiris, and while Osiris was away he gathered together seventy-two conspirators who planned to destroy Osiris. When Osiris returned they met him and invited him to a banquet where the prize was to be a splendid coffin, made to fit Osiris, although he had no idea of this. They held a great feast, and when it was over they invited all the guests to try the coffin for size. For one it was too small, for one it was too large, for one it was too short, for one it was too long. Only when Osiris got into it did it fit perfectly. Then before he had time to get out, they nailed down the top, and poured molten lead into the cracks so that he should have no air to breathe. Thus died Osiris Unifer, he who is called "Triumphant", and so he became ruler of the Dead and all who are in the West. (The Egyptians regarded the Afterworld as being in the west).

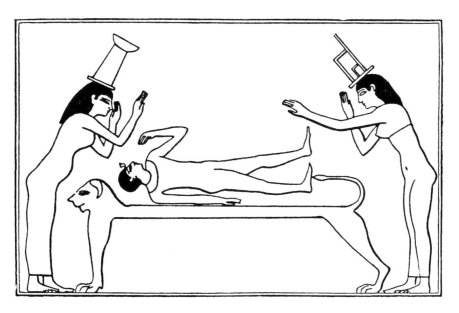

Nephthys and Isis with Osiris on his deathbed

The conspirators took the chest and placed it in the Nile where it was carried by the stream to the sea and then by currents up the coast to Byblos (near Beirut), where it landed by a tamarisk tree that grew on the shore. Then the tree who knew that a god had come to rest near it, shot out branches and grew tremendously, so that everyone wondered at its size and beauty. So much so that the King of Byblos had it cut down and used it to support the palace hall, not knowing that its branches were entwined around the coffin of Osiris.

Meanwhile in Egypt nobody knew what had happened to Osiris. Isis knew that something terrible had happened to her husband, and taking with her, her small son Horus the Younger, or Horus the Child as he was sometimes called, she fled to the Delta where she left her son with the Goddess Wadjet, the cobra goddess

Isis with the child Horus

Wadjet

of Lower Egypt, in the old grey city of Pe (Buto). Wadjet took the child and placed him in the floating island of Chemmis so that he should be safe from Seth. Then Isis set out to look for the body of her husband, for she knew that the souls of men cannot rest until the correct funeral rites are performed.

26

She wandered through the land of Egypt always asking of the children if they had seen the coffin and they told her of the painted coffer that had floated down the Nile and out onto the Great Green Waters. Forever asking the children, Isis came at last to Byblos where she sat at the mouth of the Nahr al-Kalb, the Dog River, where the maidens of the Queen of Byblos came to bathe and do the palace washing. Isis helped them and adjusted their jewels, and when they returned to the palace they were accompanied by a sweet odour, for as you may know all the deities have the most delightful smell. When the Queen asked where they had obtained the scent, the maidens replied that it had come from the sad woman seated on the shore. So the Queen went and fetched her and they talked of their children, for the small prince of Byblos was a sickly child and near to death.

Isis who was a skilled healer offered to cure the prince, if she could do so in her own way. The King and Queen agreed, and daily the small prince, Diktys, grew better and stronger. The Queen asked her handmaidens what the strange woman did, but they were unable to tell her. They said "all we know is that she goes into the hall of the pillar and we hear a strange twittering". The next night the Queen hid in the great hall to watch what Isis was doing to her son. Isis shut and barred the doors, built up the fire till it glowed red and hot, then she made a space between the logs where she placed the boy. Then she turned herself into a swallow and flew round the pillar, which she knew contained the body of Osiris, crying and lamenting. The Queen, however, was horrified at what was happening to her child; she rushed forward and snatched him from the fire, and tried to flee with him from the hall. Isis turned back into her real form and towered above the luckless Queen, who fell to her knees and offered Isis everything she possessed. Isis however wanted nothing, and said "O foolish woman, why did you take the child. In a few more days everything that was mortal in him would have been burnt away, and he would have become as the gods, forever young and immortal." Isis then asked the King and Queen to give her the pillar and what it contained; so men were brought, the pillar was taken down and split open and the coffin of Osiris revealed. Isis gave back the pillar to the people of Byblos, where it was worshipped for many years.

27

Nephthys, Osiris and Isis

28

She placed the coffin in a boat and returned to Egypt. When she got back, she hid the coffin in the Delta under a bush while she went back to Pe to see how her son Horus was getting on. She found that he had been bitten by a scorpion and had to wait until he had recovered. It was thus some time before she returned to where she had left the body of Osiris.

In the meantime, while she had been away Seth had gone hunting in the marshes for wild boar. He saw the coffin glinting in the moonlight, tore out the body and ripped it into many pieces. Some say he divided the body into fourteen pieces, others into sixteen, and then he scattered the bits throughout the land of Egypt. After he had done this he laughed and said "It is not possible to destroy the body of a god, but I have done the impossible: I have destroyed the body of Osiris."

When Isis got back she found nothing but the broken coffin and she knew Seth was responsible for it, and she had to make her weary search all over again. She made a small boat of papyrus and sailed through the marshes and up the river in search of the pieces of the body. She knew that Seth must not know what she found, or what she did with it. To confound him, whenever she found a piece of the body she built a beautiful shrine and performed the funeral rites, pretending she buried it there. Really, however, she took the pieces with her, and by using her magic powers united the broken body into its old form. Whether she buried the whole body or only part of it at Abydos is uncertain, but Abydos traditionally became the god's resting place. Here were performed annually plays in his honour, as they were in other places like Edfu and Dendera, which had shrines to Osiris. Meanwhile, Osiris remains in the Duat (Afterworld), the Judge and Ruler of the dead, until such time as he shall rise again and govern Egypt as before.

8   THE CONTENDINGS OF HORUS AND SETH
(Part I)

This account of the struggle between Horus and Seth comes from the Chester Beatty Papyrus No. 1, translated by Alan Gardiner.

The scene opens in the courtroom of the gods, where the child Horus is claiming the sovereignty of Egypt possessed by his father Osiris, who has been killed by Seth. He already seems to have acquired some of the trappings of royalty as he is wearing the White Crown of Upper Egypt, and has started to place his name in a cartouche. At this point Thoth, who supports Horus, announces the presentation of the Eye, of great religious significance, to Atum, the All God, leader of the Ennead of Helipolis. Shu, the

The Eye of Horus

God of the Air, chooses this auspicious moment to vote that the petition of Horus should be granted, and this is seconded by Thoth. Isis, delighted, asks the north wind to blow to the west and inform Osiris of this, but Atum does not agree to this somewhat precipitate action. The Ennead of Heliopolis, who are his descendants, then point out that Horus is already partly accepted, but Atum is not pleased and makes no reply.

Then Seth spoke, and appealed to the gods to cast out Horus so that he, Seth, could show his power over him. Thoth replied

30

that a fight was no way to settle a dispute, and went on to say that it would be an injustice to give the Land of Egypt to Seth, while Horus, the heir to Osiris was still alive. This annoyed Re-Harakhte who supported Seth. Atum suggested that they should send for Ba-neb-tetet, the Ram God of Mendes and should agree to abide by his decision. Ba-neb-tetet came, bringing with him Ptah-tatenen, the earth-god form of the god Ptah. Ba-neb-tetet refused to make a judgement, because he said he did not know the facts of the case. He advised the gods to write to Neith, the goddess of Sais, one of the great deities of Egypt and mother of Re, and to abide by her decision. The Nine Gods of Heliopolis then informed Ba-neb-tetet that the case between Horus and Seth had already been settled in ancient times, at the time of the Followers of Horus, in the Hall of Truth. However, no details of this judgement seem to have been made available.

The gods then ordered Thoth to write a letter to Neith. This was done and Neith replied that they must give the Land of Egypt to Horus, son of Osiris, otherwise an injustice would be done. She also threatened that if this was not done, she would cause the sky to fall down on the earth, a contingency against which the ancient Egyptians were always safeguarding themselves. She also suggested that Seth should be rewarded for the loss of Egypt by receiving two Syrian goddesses, Anat and Astarte, and some wealth. The other gods agreed that this was right but not Atum, the president of the court, who reviled Horus for being a young boy. No one disputed what he said except the god Baba who said to Re-Harakhte, "Your shrine is empty", meaning he had no position. Re-Harakhte went back to his house and sulked, until Hathor went and cheered him up. He then returned to the courtroom. One gathers that the gods were getting rather tired as this trial had already, when the story opens, been going on for some eighty years.

Horus and Seth were then called to state their case. Seth said that he was the strongest of the gods. He travelled daily in the boat of Re, and repulsed the sun god's enemies; no one else could do that. Therefore he was entitled to have Egypt. The gods agreed with him. Then Horus said it was not right that he should be defrauded of his inheritance in front of the Nine Gods. Isis lost her temper, and to soothe her the Nine Gods assured her that Horus would get his rights. This annoyed Seth, and he threatened to kill them off one at a time with his heavy sceptre.

Re-Harakhte who was tired of Isis and her interventions suggested to the court that it should cross over to an island in the river and have lunch and give judgement there. Anti, the ferryman, was told not to take Isis across. Isis disguised herself as an old woman and bribed Anti with her gold ring to take her across. When there, she transformed herself into a beautiful girl whom Seth saw and fell in love with. When he made advances to her she told him a story of how she was the wife of a cattle herder who had died, but that she had born him a son. In the course of time a stranger had come and sat down in the cattle byre and threatened to beat her son and carry off the cattle. She asked Seth to help her against the man. Then Seth said "Shall the cattle be given to strangers while the son of the farmer exists", so that his actions were condemned out of his own mouth. When Seth found that he had been tricked by Isis, he told the court the whole story and Re-Harakhte said "You have passed judgement on yourself, what is there for you to do next?"

Tired of the court, the Nine Gods journeyed to the Western Delta and sat down on a small hill. Re-Harakhte and Atum sent to ask why they were doing nothing, and suggested that they must want Horus and Seth to spend their whole lives in and out of court. Re-Harakhte and Atum then commanded the Nine Gods to set again the White Crown on the head of Horus. Seth was furious. He challenged Horus to an underwater contest with both of them in the form of hippopotami. Isis anxious to help Horus made a harpoon of copper and cast it into the water where they were, but it hit Horus instead of Seth and he cried out in anguish, whereupon Isis using her magic powers withdrew the harpoon. Then she threw it once more and it pierced Seth, and he cried out, and she was sorry for him, for after all he was her brother, so she released him from the harpoon.

Then Horus was very angry with Isis for setting Seth free, and so he came out of the water and cut off her head with an axe, and clasping the head went up into the mountains. Isis turned herself into a flint headless statue. Horus then went off to the Khargah and Dakhlah oases to escape the gods who wished to punish him for murdering his mother. He lay down under a bush, where Seth found him and gouged out his two eyes, which he set up to light the desert area where he was. He then went back to the gods and said that he had been unable to find Horus anywhere. Meanwhile the blind Horus had been found by Hathor, who restored his sight by pouring milk into his eyes. Hathor then went to the gods and reported what Seth had done.

Seth

The two gods Horus and Seth were then ordered to appear before the Nine Gods and Re-Harakhte, who told them that everyone was tired of their behaviour and that they would have to make it up. Seth then offered to hold a feast for Horus who accepted; he then got drunk and was assaulted by Seth. He was rescued by Isis, and after Seth had been discredited it was decided to write to Osiris asking his opinion. Osiris was by now thoroughly tired of all this toing and froing and sent a message to say that the land where he was, was full of dog-headed messengers, who were not afraid of any god, and if they did not settle the dispute immediately he would send them out to destroy the gods. The gods therefore immediately confirmed Horus in the place of his father, set the White Crown for the third time on his head, and imprisoned Seth. So ended the Contendings of Horus and Seth.

The battle between Horus and Seth for the mastery of Egypt took many years and several forms - a physical war as well as a court case. The account given here is from the texts to be found on the walls of the Ptolemaic temple to Horus the Behedet at Edfu.

According to this story the battle began in the three hundredth and sixty-third year of the reign of Re-Harakhte upon earth, because as all Egyptians knew the gods ruled in Egypt in prehistoric times before the kings took over. The people were conspiring against Re in the Southland at this time, so Re sailed down river in his boat and arrived at Edfu (Apollinopolis) with Horus in the boat with him. And Horus flew up to heaven in the shape of a great winged sun-disc which men try to paint over the gates of their temples to this day. The colours were those of the sunset mingled with those of the Nile, and they represented the plumage of Horus, "the god of the dappled plumage". Horus pursued his enemies in the form of a great winged disc and attacked them so that none whom he came across were left alive. Then Thoth said to Horus, "You are the Great Protector", and for this reason the boat of Horus is called *mak-a*, the great protector, to this day. But this was the first battle and the last great battle was not yet.

Then the enemies of Re transformed themselves into crocodiles and hippopotami, and attacked the boat of Re as it sailed upon the water, and Horus hastened to their help with all his men armed with harpoons. Because of this, he is known as "Horus the Harpooner" to this day. And opposite the city of Edfu were slain on this day, six hundred and fifty-one of these animals. But this was the second battle and the last great battle was not yet.

34

Then Horus the Behedet drove his enemies southwards and destroyed them in a region of the south-east and many were killed but others escaped to the Northland. And he caught them to the north-east of Dendera and made a great slaughter with his weapons of iron and his spears and axes. And the courage of his enemies wavered before him, and they fled to the Northland among the swamps and papyrus. This was in the territory of Heben. And though many were destroyed, many escaped, and the last great battle was not yet.

And the enemies rose up before him on the lake of the north and their faces were set towards the Great Green Waters (the Mediterranean). The Majesty of Re said to Horus, "Behold these enemies have assembled on the Western Water of the nome of Mert to band themselves together with the enemies who serve Seth who are in this place." And Horus beseeched Re to let him go against the enemies in the boat of Re, and he made an assault upon them on the bank of the lake, and he made a great massacre among them, and he captured many of them to the number of three hundred and eighty-one enemies and he gave them to his followers. But the last great battle was not yet.

Then Seth raged against Horus like a cheetah of the South because Horus had killed one of his main allies. Seth roared against heaven and his voice was as the voice of thunder, and to escape Horus he changed into a great snake and disappeared into the earth. Nobody saw him do this, or marked where he went. But the gods who know all things knew he had done this and planned to obstruct his return to the earth. Meanwhile Seth's associates knowing that he was alive took comfort and assembled again and filled their boats which were on the canal. Then Horus went against them in the boat of Re. He changed himself into a great winged disc and flew over the marshes. When he saw the enemy gathered together in one place, he attacked them and routed them, for Horus enjoyed a day of battle to a day of feasting. And to this day men hold ceremonies in remembrance of the Battles of Horus on the first day of the first appearing of the inundation, and on the seventh day of the first appearing of the mounds after the inundation. And the waters where Horus sought and defeated Seth's followers are called to this day the "Waters of Seeking", because it was here that Horus sought his foes. And this battle was in the North but the last great battle was not yet.

Then Horus sent out his followers, and they hunted down the enemy, and they captured many prisoners, one hundred and six from the east, and the same number from the west, and they were slain before Re as a sacrifice. Then Re gave to his followers two cities for their own use, and they were called thereafter the Mesen cities. In the shrines of these cities the sacred rites of Horus were performed four days in every year.

Again the enemies massed themselves against Horus, and this time he transformed himself into a fierce lion, and in this form he defeated his enemies and took many captives. Then they went north until they reached the shores of the Great Green (the sea), and here the waves of the sea broke on the shore with a noise like thunder. Then Thoth rose from his place in the boat of Re and uttered spells and chanted, and the wind ceased and peace fell on the waters. No enemies were in sight so that Re and his followers and Horus went southwards, and with haste they sailed to Ta-Kens "the Land of the Bow", which is now known as Nubia. Then Horus changed himself back into a great winged disc and he was accompanied by the goddesses of the South and the North in the form of two cobras with their crowns upon their heads. Now this was the encounter between Horus and the enemies of Re in the Southland, but the last great battle was not yet.

Then Re came in his boat and he commanded that men should carve the winged disc above the temple doors that men might remember in what form Horus had hunted on his behalf and slain the enemy.

Now some say that the battles of Horus and Seth are over and that the triumph was with Horus, and after this Osiris will return to rule upon the earth. But others say that the last battle is still to come, and that until Seth is killed there will be no peace upon the earth.

This is the tale of what happened according to those who thought that the war was over and that Horus was the victor. By this time the young Horus, son of Osiris, had grown to manhood, whereupon Seth issued a challenge to him before Re, and Horus and his followers came forth in their boats, with their glittering

Horus the Younger on a lotus

weapons of iron. The boat was decorated by Isis with gold upon the prow, and she said to Horus, "You will be victorious for you are fighting for the throne of your father, and I am with you." Then Seth assumed the form of a great red hippopotamus and he with his followers travelled from the Northland to the Southland. When he arrived at Elephantine, he rose and cursed Horus, whereupon a great wind rose up and a raging tempest. His words were like thunder in the sky and they rolled from the southern heavens back to the northern heavens, and at once a fierce storm broke out over the boats of Horus, and the wind roared and waves rose and the boats tossed like straws and to this day this part of the river is the most dangerous with sudden storms and high waves. Through the darkness of the storm shone the prow of the boat of Horus with the golden ornaments that Isis had placed there. Then Horus took upon himself the likeness of a young man, and his height was eight cubits and he held a harpoon in his hand and its length was four cubits (one cubit equals 22 inches). Over his head he brandished the weapon as though it was only a reed and cast it at the great red hippopotamus who was waiting in the shallows for the boats to sink in the storm. At the first throw the weapon struck the head of the great red hippopotamus and sank deep into his brain. Thus died Seth, the enemy of Horus, Seth the Wicked One who had murdered Osiris.

To this day the priests of Horus at Edfu, and the kings' daughters, and the women of Busiris, and the women of Pe, chant a hymn and strike the drum for Horus in triumph. This is their song: "Rejoice O women of Busiris! Rejoice O women of Pe! Horus has overthrown his enemies! Exalt dwellers in Edfu! Horus the Great Lord of Heaven has smitten his enemies and the enemy of his father. Eat the flesh of the vanquished, drink his blood, burn his bones in the fire. Let him be cut to pieces and his bones given to the cats and the rest to the reptiles. O Horus the Striker, the Great One of Valour, Chief of the Gods, the Harpooner, the Hero, the son of his Father, Horus of Edfu, Horus the Avenger! He has destroyed the wicked one, he has made a whirlpool of the blood of his enemy, his shaft has made its prey. Behold Horus at the prow of his boat, like Re he shines on the horizon. He is decked in green linen, in binding linen, in fine linen and byssus. The double diadem is on his head. The two serpents are on his brow. O Horus the Avenger (of his father). Your harpoon is of metal, the shaft is of the sycamore of the desert, the net is woven by Hathor of the Roses. You have aimed to the right, you have cast to the left, we give praise to you to the height of heaven, for you have destroyed the wickedness of your enemy. We give praise to you, we worship your majesty, O Horus of Edfu, Horus the Avenger."

10   *HORUS AND THE BLACK PIG*

This legend is known to us from Chapter 112 of the *Book of the Dead* called 'Knowing the Souls of Pe'.

"I know the reason why the city of Pe was given to Horus and I will tell you." These words were said to have been spoken by an inhabitant of Pe when asked why the city of Pe was in the possession of Horus. It had not always been so, for originally it had belonged to Djbaut, the old heron god. The word *pe* means seat or throne, and Pe was always connected with the Predynastic capital of Lower Egypt, a place where many of the royal customs that were used throughout Egypt had their beginning. Re gave Horus Pe because of the injury to his eye.

Now between Horus and Seth there was always enmity and strife, and the struggle continued between them. Seth was clever and devious and tried to win by craft and deceit, but Horus only worked through truth and righteousness. He had blue eyes and many sought to know the future by gazing into his blue eyes. One day Re decided to consult with Horus, and this seemed to Seth a good moment to do Horus some harm. Therefore, he took upon himself the likeness of a Black Pig, very fierce and large. Then Re met Horus and asked him if he could consult him about the future by gazing into his eyes. When he gazed on the eyes of Horus, their colour was greenish-blue like that of the Great Green Waters when the summer sun shines on them. While Re was gazing at Horus, the Black Pig passed by, but neither Re nor Horus knew that it was Seth. Then Re called out to Horus "Look at that Black Pig! Never have I seen one so large and fierce."

So Horus looked at the Pig but he was not prepared to protect himself, for he did not know it was Seth. He thought it was a large boar from the thickets of the marshes of the North Country. Then Seth aimed a beam of fire, and he realised it was Seth and said, "It is Seth, and he has wounded me with fire in the eye."

But Seth had gone and the large Black Pig was never seen again; it had done its work. So Re cursed the pig because of Seth and he said "Let the pig be an abomination to Horus." Then Re, who was also a great physician as well as a creator god said "Let him (Horus) be placed on his bed and he shall recover." And to this day the followers of Horus sacrifice the pig at full moon to Horus in memory of what Seth did to him.

The Souls of Pe

Then Horus said to Re "Give me two brethren of the City of Pe and two brethren of the City of Neken, who shall be with me as everlasting judges" and it was done and forever after these were the judges of Egypt. Not only judges were given to Horus, but the City of Pe as well. And when the eye of Horus healed, Horus rejoiced, and the earth blossomed, and the rain ceased, and all was well in the land of Egypt.

40

11 THE SCORPIONS OF ISIS

This is a spell for scorpion bites and comes from the Metternich stele found by workmen digging a cistern in Alexandria in 1828. This is the text in part, and it is written as if Isis herself was speaking.

"I am Isis, Mistress of Magic and Speaker of Spells. I came out of the House of Seth, and Thoth advised me to go and hide myself in the Marshlands of Lower Egypt, with my small son Horus. I was accompanied by my seven scorpions. They guarded me wherever I went; Tefen and Befen were behind me, Mestet and Mestetef were on either side of me, and Petet, Thetet and Matet went in front of me to open the way. I spoke loudly to them and said, 'Go always ahead, do not look to the right or to the left and do not attack children or any poor defenceless people or animals.'

Then they led me to the City of *Per Swi* where the Papyrus Marshes begin, the city of the Two Goddesses of the Divine Sandals. Here I would have liked to have rested because I had travelled a long way and I was wayworn and weary. However, the first house at which I stopped, the woman called Gloria was afraid of the scorpions and shut the door in my face. I went on further into the town and found a house belonging to one of the marsh-women who consented to receive me.

The scorpions were annoyed that I had not been able to rest where I wished to, and as a result they consulted together and decided to take action. They came and put all their poison on the sting of the scorpion Tefen, so that his sting had seven-fold power. He then returned to the first house where I had stopped, and because the door did not fit very well was able to crawl in and sting the son of the house with a poison of seven-fold power. The child became very ill and fire broke out in the house. Gloria

41

The Metternich Stele (Obverse)

rushed round the town asking for help, but received none. I, Isis, meanwhile repented of what had been done and called the woman to me. I went with her to her house and laid hands on the child, because I am Isis, Mistress of Magic, Speaker of Spells. I called on the poison to leave him, 'O poison of Tefen, enter not into him, come fall upon the ground. O poison of Befen, come forth and fall upon the ground. O poison of Mestet, go no further, come forth and fall upon the ground. O poison of Mestetef, go no further, come forth and fall upon the ground, for I am Isis, Mistress of Magic and Speaker of Spells. O poison of Petet, proceed no further, come forth and fall upon the ground. Poison of Thetet and Matet, rise not, do not enter into him but come forth. The child shall live, the poison will die because my father Geb has given me control over all reptiles. As truly as Horus lives for his mother, so this child will live for his mother.' Then the fire in the house was extinguished and the child was cured.''

To this day people who are stung by scorpions have a poultice made of barley bread placed on the wound which draws out the poison if the name of Isis, Mistress of Magic and Speaker of Spells is invoked.

12 HOW ISIS OBTAINED THE SECRET NAME OF RE

This text is to be found in the Papyrus of Turin, plates 31 to 77 and 131 to 138.

Re, the King of the Gods had many names and many aspects. His secret name was known only to himself and not to the other gods, as this secret name contained his hidden power. Now Isis was the mistress of magic, and she wished to become as powerful as Re himself, but in order to become so she had to know his written name. Now it happens that though the gods cannot die they can age, and Re had become an old man, his skin was like ivory and his hair likewise, and when he sat on his throne of the Horizons he often slept and his spittle dribbled onto the earth. Now the gods can only be hurt by their own creations, and as Re was so powerful he could only be injured by something that contained his own strength. Therefore Isis who changed herself into the likeness of a woman, moulded a serpent (viper) out of the dust and the saliva from Re's mouth. She then placed this magic serpent on the path that Re would tread when he went daily through the Two Lands of Egypt, as was his wont.

The god arose and went on his way and when he reached the serpent, it put forth his tongue and bit him. And fire consumed the body of Re and he was unable to speak, his whole body shook with the power of the poison that was in the serpent's bite. The god then pulled himself together and spoke to the gods around him asking them to help him. He told them that he had been wounded by a deadly thing, which he had not created. He asked the other gods for help, and asked that they should bring before him all who had magical powers that they might aid him.

Then his children, the other gods, came to him weeping, and the goddess Isis came and asked him what the matter was. She said

44

Re

"What has happened O Divine Father? Tell me who has done this to you. Was it a serpent that you created who reared his head against you? If so I shall destroy it with my spells." Then the Great God Re answered her and said, "I was journeying through the Two Lands as is my custom, to see all that I have created, when I was bitten by a serpent that I did not see. It was not fire. It was not water. I am colder than water, I am hotter than fire. My limbs are drenched with sweat. I shiver, my eyes cannot see clearly and I drip as though it was the heart of summer." Isis then said to Re "O Divine Father, tell me your secret name", and Re answered "I am the maker of heaven and earth, I have tied the mountains together and created all things. I am the maker of moisture. I have made heaven and the two horizons. I have created the gods, and I have made light and darkness. I am he who causes the Nile to rise, and I am he whose name the gods do not know. I am the opener of the year. I am Khepre in the morning, I am Re at noonday, and Atum in the evening." Isis said to Re, "Your name is not mentioned in all the things you have named. Tell me what it is, and the poison will cease to trouble you." Then Re agreed to tell her his name, which he did in secret away from the other gods, so that no one else should know of it. Then Isis spoke to the poison, and told it to come out of the body of Re, and it did so. Re was cured, but Isis knew his secret name and thus had power over him.

45

13   KING KHUFU AND THE MAGICIANS

These are three popular tales found in the Westcar Papyrus now in Berlin. Traditionally they were stories told to the king while he was watching the building of the Great Pyramid. Two of the stories deal with previous times, the last is an account of the future.

THE WIFE OF THE LECTOR PRIEST

This is the earliest of the stories told to Khufu and dates to the time of King Zozer of the Third Dynasty. This story was told to Khufu by Prince Khafre. It happened when King Zozer came to Memphis to the temple of Ptah. Here he took the chief lector priest with him called Ubaoner. Now the wife of Ubaoner was in love with a townsman, and in the garden of Ubaoner was a lake and a pavilion beside it. The townsman, who is nameless, said to the wife, let us go and enjoy ourselves in the pavilion by the lake, and they did so, passing the day in drinking. In the evening the townsman went for a swim in the lake and the whole affair was observed by the house steward. When his master returned after many days, this official reported it to Ubaoner who was, like all lector priests, a magician. And he sent for his staff of office of ebony and gold and he made a crocodile of wax and put a spell over it and said "Whoever comes to bathe in my lake do you seize him and hold him." Then Ubaoner told the steward that when the townsman went to bathe in the lake to throw in the wax crocodile,

46

which was lifesize, behind him. Then the next time the lector priest was called away by his duties and the wife and the townsman passed a happy day in the lake pavilion, the steward watched what they did, and in the evening when the townsman went to bathe he threw in the wax crocodile behind him, and it became a real reptile and it seized the townsman in its jaws and went down to the bottom of the lake.

Now Ubaoner was away for seven days with the King and all the time the townsman was at the bottom of the lake without breathing. And when Ubaoner returned he told the King of all that had happened, and together they went to the lake and Ubaoner called to the crocodile, and it came and the King was afraid of it because it was so large. So Ubaoner took it in his hands and it became again a crocodile of wax. Then Ubaoner asked the King to pass judgement on the pair of lovers, and the King told the crocodile to take what belonged to him, and he did, and no one saw where he went. Then the King took the wife and had her taken to a field north of the Royal Residence where she was burnt alive and her ashes scattered in the Nile.

Upon hearing this story King Khufu ordered that an offering of bread and beer, flesh and fowl should be made to the *Ka* of King Zozer and a smaller offering for the soul of the lector priest.

KING SNEFRU'S DIVERSION

The second story was told by Prince Baufre and dates to the time of Snefru, the father of Khufu. One day King Snefru was wandering around the palace in search of rest and relaxation and found none. So he sent for the chief lector priest and told him that he needed to be amused and have some relaxation. The lector priest advised him to take a boat to the palace lake and to get all the most beautiful girls of the royal harem to row for him. So Snefru called for twenty oars of ebony plated with gold and twenty beautiful virgins, and he clothed them in fish-nets instead of their clothes and proceeded to row up and down the lake admiring the banks and the nesting places for fowl.

The stroke oar who was wearing a beautiful pendant of turquoise dropped it in the water. She stopped rowing immediately, and so did the girls behind her. When His Majesty asked what had happened they replied that they had stopped rowing because the stroke had done so, and she had stopped because she had dropped her turquoise fish in the lake. The King wished her to proceed and said to her, "Row on, I will replace your ornament", but

Fish pendant

the girl replied she did not want a replacement but preferred her own ornament. Then the King who wished to go on with his boating party sent for the chief lector priest, who was something of a magician. When the King explained what had happened, the lector priest spoke his words and part of the lake rose up and piled itself on the rest so that the lake bed was revealed, and the pendant was seen lying on a sherd of pottery. This he returned to its owner and the water returned to its place. The King was delighted and gave a feast to the whole palace.

King Khufu was also delighted by the story and he ordered offerings to be made for the *Ka* of King Snefru and a gift of bread and beer and incense to be given to the chief lector priest who was still alive.

THE CHILDREN OF RE

The third story deals with the future and was told to King Khufu by Djedi a magician who lived at Dashûr. He was brought to the King by Prince Hardedef who found him resting in his house with servants rubbing his feet, for he was an old man. The King asked why he had never seen him before and Djedi rightly replied he would have come had he been asked. First he was asked if he could restore the dead to life, and he said yes. The King wished to bring a captive in and have him executed but Djedi refused to practise his skills on a man and asked for a goose. This was done, the head of the goose was cut off and placed on the other side of the audience chamber, and when Djedi said certain words the two were joined together. He did this with another bird and then with an ox.

Then the King asked about the Sacred Book of Thoth, but though Djedi knew where it was, he refused to bring it to the King, saying it would not be revealed until later, when it would be brought by one of the three children of Ruddedet, who was the wife of one of the priests of Re. These children were said to have been conceived by Re, and it was foretold they would take the throne of Egypt after the death of Khufu's grandson. When the time of the birth drew near the gods decided to assist. They were sent for by Re, and were Isis, Nephthys, Khnum and the goddesses of birth Meskhenet and Heket. The gods and goddesses set out disguised as dancing girls with Khnum as their porter. Three children were born, beautiful to see with hair of lapis lazuli. The deities were paid by the priest for their assistance with a sack of barley, in which they placed musical instruments - some say three royal crowns - which made the sack so heavy that they asked if they could leave it behind under seal until they came again. So the deities went on their way. After fourteen days Ruddedet wanted some beer, but the maid told her that there was no barley left to brew beer except for the sack left by the dancers. So Ruddedet told the maid to take some from the sack and it would be replaced later. When the maid went into the storeroom she heard the sound of music, singing and shouting, and she went and told all she had heard to Ruddedet, who examined the sack and found that the

49

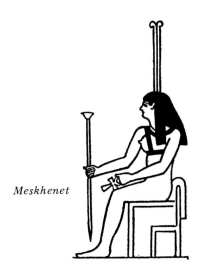

Meskhenet

music came from there. After some time Ruddedet had a quarrel with the maid and struck her. The maid was very annoyed and decided to go and tell the King of the strange happenings that had taken place in the priest's house, and how she thought three divine beings had been born to Ruddedet. So she left the house and found her elder half-brother busy in the flax field and told him what she was about to do. He was not pleased and beat her and said she should not involve her family in such an affair. After the beating the maid went to draw a bucket of water from the canal and was snatched by a crocodile. When the half-brother went to tell Ruddedet of the affair he found her weeping because she thought that the maid had gone to the palace to tell the King, and that they would all be destroyed, but the brother told her instead of the death of the maid seized by the crocodile. Thus it was that the children of Re were saved to come to the throne in due course.

14 THE STORY OF SINHUE

This tale is of Middle Kingdom date. There are various versions as it was a
popular story. The two principal texts are in the Berlin Museum (Pap. Berlin
3022 and Pap. Berlin 10499), both Middle Kingdom. There is an incomplete
copy on an ostracon (written on pottery) in the Ashmolean Museum dating to
the Nineteenth Dynasty.

Sinhue was an attendant of Nefru the wife of Senusert I and
daughter of Amenemhat I. Sinhue was at Lisht (then called Khen-
emsut, the pyramid of Senusert) when Amenemhat died. The co-
regent Senusert was on a campaign against the Libyans, from which
he was returning with captives and booty. The palace officials sent
to tell him that his father had died, and he returned immediately,
leaving the army without informing anyone. However, the other
royal sons had also been informed and some of them arrived at the
royal residence before him. Sinhue expected that there would be
trouble over the accession and if this was so, expected that he
would suffer. He therefore fled from the court. He went through
the desert till he came to the region of the quartzite quarries at the
Gebel Ahmah. He crossed the "Walls of the Ruler" at night. He
then began to cross the Desert of Sinai and almost died of thirst.
He was saved by a troop of Bedouin who had been down to Egypt
and who gave him water and milk. He went with them, and the
ruler of Upper Retinu (Syria) sent for him and asked him why he
had fled from Egypt. Sinhue replied with a series of half-truths
admitting the death of Amenemhat but not admitting that he had
been afraid of a conspiracy to keep Senusert off the throne. Sinhue
therefore remained with the Prince of Retinu who helped him and
married him to his eldest daughter. He was allotted good land in
Yaa. It was a land of figs, grapes, honey, oil and barley with all

51

kinds of cattle. He was near the desert and wild game was caught for him daily. He had wine, cooked meat, cooked fowl and fresh bread daily. He kept open house and received the Egyptian envoys on their journey to Syria. His children grew up and became heads of their tribes. Then the local people became jealous of his success and one of the champions came to challenge him to personal combat. This Sinhue won, shooting him in the neck with an arrow and cutting his head off with an axe. He received all the champion's cattle and goods, stripping all that was in his tent. Sinhue therefore became rich. He was not happy because as he grew older his thoughts turned to Egypt, and he wished to return home.

He therefore sent a message to King Senusert who in reply sent him royal gifts and a Royal Decree. This admitted that there was no case against Sinhue, that he had gone off to the foreign countries of his own free will and asking him to come back to Egypt. It asked him to think of the day of burial. It said in part "You shall not die abroad. Nor shall the Asiatics bury you. You shall not be wrapped in a sheep's hide as a coffin. Too long have you been wandering the world away from Egypt. Come home, think of your dead body." Sinhue was delighted to receive the document and danced and shouted for joy. He wrote back admitting he had fled in fear, what of, he did not admit. He said he would return as soon as he had disposed of all he had in Yaa. He handed over all his possessions to his eldest son and went south to Egypt. He paused at the "Ways of Horus" (the string of fortresses that line the north coast of Sinai between Egypt and Palestine).

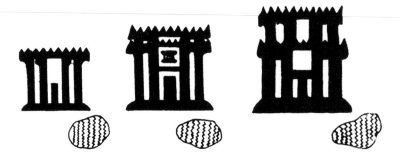

"The Ways of Horus"

The commander of the fortresses sent a messenger to the Egyptian court to say that he had arrived. Then the Egyptian King sent a trusted overseer of the Royal Domains to meet him, and gifts for the Asiatics that had accompanied him. He then set out for the city of Itj-tawy, where the court was. Here His Majesty was seated in a golden kiosk, Sinhue prostrated himself, but he did not know in what part of the world he was as he was so overcome with emotion. "I did not know myself, my *Ba* was gone, my limbs trembled, when this god addressed me." Then His Majesty spoke to the courtiers and said "Lift him up and let him speak." The members of the royal family came in but they did not recognise him as he was dressed as an Asiatic. Then His Majesty made him a Companion among the Nobles and sent him to the robing rooms so that he might be dressed as an Egyptian. He was bathed and cleansed, and the years rolled from him. He was shaved and his hair washed and combed. For the first time in years he saw himself in a mirror. He was clothed in fine linen and his body anointed with oil. He returned his clothes to the Land of the Sand-dwellers, and the cedar oil to those who like it. He was given a house and land. A burial place was constructed for him and everything was done for his funeral. "I was in favour with the King until the day of my departing."

It is not known where this papyrus was found in Egypt but it turned up in the Hermitage Museum in Petrograd (now Leningrad) and was deciphered by the Russian Egyptologist, W. Golenischeff, who presented it to the Orientalists Congress held in Berlin in 1881. He then published a translation in French in Leipzig the same year. Since then it has been translated into German, French and English. The date of the original story is probably Twelfth Dynasty, that is about 1800 B.C.

It is a story within a story and begins with the arrival at Elephantine (Aswan) of a ship containing the captain of a vessel which had been lost on government service in Wawat, part of Nubia. The dispossessed captain was lurking in his cabin when the captain of the boat came to tell him that they had arrived safely. However, he did not want to know as he was afraid that when he went to tell the king of his misfortunes and losses ti. he would be executed. To cheer him up the ship's captain told him a story of what happened once to him.

The captain said, "May your heart be cheerful my lord, for we have arrived at the country of Egypt. My sailors have driven home the mooring stakes, the vessel is attached to the shore safely, the offerings to the gods have been made. We have lost none of our sailors although we went to the furthest parts of Wawat, and we have returned in peace. Wash yourself and prepare for the audience with the king. Speak to him freely, tell him what is in your heart and thus you may escape the veiling of the face (a reference to the face of the criminal being covered at his execution). Appease the wrath of the king and you may be all right."

"Now I will relate a similar adventure that happened to me, when I went to the mines of the king. I went down in a ship over one hundred feet in length and thirty feet wide, and it carried five hundred sailors of the best of the land of Egypt. They who had seen the earth, who had seen the sky and who were bolder of heart than lions. They were persuaded that the high wind would not come, that disaster would not befall, but a high wind arose when we were in the open, and before we could reach land, the gale increased, so that the waves were 30 feet high. I seized a plank, and as for the ship it sank, and of those on board not one was left. As for me I was washed up upon an island, and this was only because a wave of the sea threw me up upon the shore. I spent the night in a tree, afraid of wild animals, and the next three days wandered about looking for human habitation. I found on the island, figs, grapes, berries and seeds, wonderful leeks, melons and cucumbers, as well as birds and fish. In fact I wanted for nothing except human companionship. I then took a stick, and with the help of some dried bark made myself a fire and made a burnt sacrifice to the gods. After I had done this I heard a voice like thunder, and I thought the sea was getting up again. The trees shivered, the earth trembled, I flung myself on the ground, and when I recovered consciousness I saw an immense serpent, over one hundred feet long, and with a great tail. All his body shone as though it was covered with gold, and his eyebrows were as if they had been inlaid with real lapis lazuli. And he opened his mouth and said to me, "Who has brought you here vassal, who has brought you here? If you do not

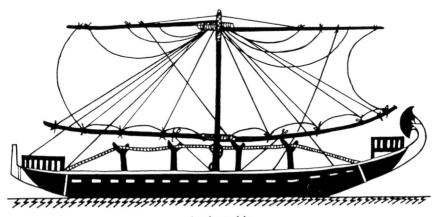

Ancient ship

answer truly I will reduce you to ashes, and make you as if you had never been." Now I was alarmed, and I lay on my face in front of this snake, and I was so afraid that I lost consciousness and could not speak. Then he took me in his mouth, and carried me to his lair very gently without breaking any of my bones.

Then as I still lay without speaking, he turned to me and said, "Who has brought you? Who has brought you, vassal, to this island, the shores of which are bathed by the great green sea?" And I replied to him, "I am one who was going to the mines on a mission from my sovereign the King of Egypt, in a ship over one hundred feet in length and thirty feet wide, accompanied by five hundred sailors, the best of the land of Egypt. They had seen the earth, they had seen the sky, they were braver of heart than lions. They were persuaded that the gale would not come, that the sea would not rise, but when we were in the open sea a storm got up, the waves rose to thirty feet high, and the vessel broke up, and they were all drowned. Only I was saved because I took hold of a plank, and with its help, I was driven by the waves to the island." The serpent said to me, "Do not be afraid, do not look so miserable. If you have come to me it is because God has permitted you to survive, and that he has led you to this island of the *Ka* (Double) which is full of good things. Behold you will wait here for four months, and then a boat will pass by, and you will know some of the crew, and you will go with them back to your own land, and to your own city. When sorrows are over, it is delightful to tell of them. I am here with my brothers and my children to the number of seventy-five, and a girl who came when the star fell." (This seems to refer to the fall of a meteorite). And I stretched myself on my face and I said to him, "I shall describe all this to the king, and I shall cause him to know of your greatness and your goodness to me. And I shall bring to you incense and myrrh, and perfumes, and offerings, and burnt sacrifices of animals and birds." And he laughed and said, "Use your eyes, can you not see that all the things that you have promised me I have here already in abundance on the island. But anyway I shall not be here to receive them, as after you have gone the great green sea will cover this place, and it will be as if it had never been."

The serpent was quite right. The ship came as he had said after four months, and I watched it approach seated on a high tree, and I recognised some of the crew. Then I went at once to tell the serpent the good news. And he said "Good luck, good luck vassal, you will go home and find all is well in your city and in your house, and these are my gifts for you." And he gave me incense, myrrh, perfumes and spices, pepper, antimony, hippopotamus tails, tusks of ivory, greyhounds, apes and giraffes and all excellent things. And I loaded them all on the ship, and I made a last offering to the serpent who had made me a rich man with all this merchandise, and I set sail for home. And after two months I returned to the land of Egypt, and I told my story to the King of Egypt, and I presented to him the gifts of the serpent, and he made of me one of his officers, and so I have remained to the present day. Surely my adventures will reassure you."

But the captain who had lost his ship seemed to be unimpressed, "You cannot help me my friend", he said, "who gives water to a goose on the day it is to be killed?"

So that now the writing is finished from beginning to end, and this is how it was found on the papyrus. He who has written it is the scribe of clever fingers, Amun-Amanu.

This is a true account of the life of a naval officer from el-Kab, the ancient city of Nekheb, in the early years of the Eighteenth Dynasty, who served his rulers for nearly fifty years. It is inscribed on the rock-cut tomb chapel at el-Kab, on the right wall of the chamber, and has been published several times by Breasted in *Ancient Records* Vol. II, 1-16 and 38-39, and Pritchard, *Ancient Near Eastern Texts*, 233-34. It dates from the sixteenth century B.C.

The commander Ahmose, son of Abana his mother, justified, said, "I speak to let you know what favours were granted to me. I received the Gold of Valour (the gold flies) many times. I received male and female slaves and many fields. My name was put forward as a brave man which will always be known in the land of Egypt.

I grew up in the town of Nekheb. My father Baba, son of Reonet, was a soldier of the King of Upper and Lower Egypt, Seqenenre, justified, Tao II of the Seventeenth Dynasty. I became a soldier in his place on the ship *The Wild Bull*, in the time of the Lord of the Two Lands, Nebpehtire, the founder of the Eighteenth Dynasty. I was still a youth, before I had taken a wife.

When I had established a household I was transferred to the ship *Northern* because I had a good record. I used to accompany the King on foot when he was in his chariot. When the town of Avaris, the Hyksos capital, was besieged, I showed bravery in front of His Majesty. I was therefore appointed to the ship *Rising in Memphis*. Then there was fighting in the canal 'Pedku' of Avaris. I killed a man and cut off his hand. When this was reported to the Royal Herald he gave me my first Gold of Valour. Then there was further fighting and again I took a hand. I was given the Gold of Valour a second time.

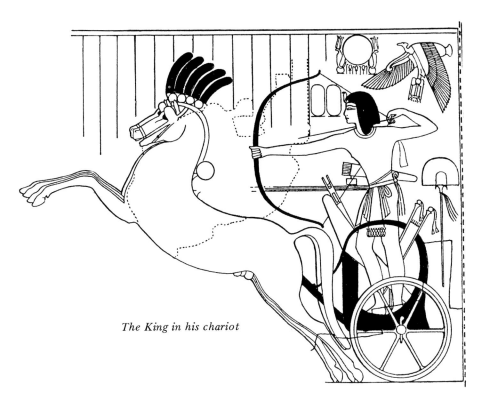

The King in his chariot

Then there was fighting south of the town, and I took a man as a living prisoner. This I did by going down into the water and capturing him on the city side, and then crossing the water carrying him. Again report was made to the Royal Herald and I was awarded the Gold of Valour a third time. Avaris was sacked and I took as booty one man and three women, and His Majesty gave them to me as slaves.

I was at the siege of Sharuhen (probably Tell el-Far'ah) for three years. In the sack I made captive two women and a hand, and received the Gold of Valour for the fourth time. My captives were given to me as slaves.

After His Majesty had destroyed the Asiatics, he went southwards to attack the Nubian nomads. He went to Khent-en-Nefer in the region of the Second Cataract. His Majesty made a great slaughter amongst the Nubian Bowmen, and I brought off from there as

59

spoil, two living captives and three hands. I was rewarded with the Gold of Valour for the fifth time.

Then one named Aata came to the South and he brought on his own doom. His Majesty found him at Tent-taa, a place in Kush. His Majesty carried him off and kept his people as living booty. I captured two young warriors from the ship Aata. Then I was given five persons and a portion of land in my own town. The same was done for the rest of the crew. Then came an enemy called Tetian, an Egyptian, who had rebelled against His Majesty. He was destroyed and his followers likewise. I got three slaves as my share, and some more land.

Next, I travelled south with King Djeserkare Amenhotep I, justified, when he sailed to Kush to enlarge the borders of Egypt. His Majesty smote the Nubian Bowmen, they were destroyed and placed in fetters. I was in the van of the army and I was fighting very well. His Majesty saw my work: I carried off a living captive and gave him to the King. I brought back the King on my ship to Egypt. I also brought back two other female captives as well as those whom I had presented to His Majesty. Then I was promoted and made a 'Warrior of the Ruler'.

After the death of the King, I accompanied his successor, King Akheperkare Tuthmosis I, south to Khent-en-Nefer to crush rebellion throughout the Lands of the South. I helped him repel the incursions from the desert areas. I was brave in towing the ship through the cataract, and so I was made a commander. Then His Majesty was informed that the Nubians had attacked us again and he became enraged. He became like a cheetah of the South; he shot his arrows at the foe and they pierced the chests of his attackers. Then the foe turned to flee as they could not stand against the wearer of the Uraeus. A great slaughter was made among the Nubian Bowmen, and their dependents were carried off captive to Egypt. His Majesty journeyed northwards into Egypt and landed at Iput-isut, Karnak, to the north of Thebes, having subdued the Nine Bows, the enemies of Egypt.

After this Tuthmosis I and I went forth to Retinu, to assuage his heart in the foreign countries. His Majesty reached Naharain and found the enemy while they were not yet ready for battle. As

60

a result His Majesty made of them a great slaughter. He took count-less living captives. I was in the van of the army and His Majesty saw my bravery. I captured a chariot, its horse, and he who was in it, as a living captive. When these were presented to His Majesty, I was once again given the Gold of Valour, the sixth time.

Now I have reached old age. Favoured as before, I shall go to rest in the tomb that I have made."

This account of the birth of Hatshepsut of the Eighteenth Dynasty is to be found on the north side of the second terrace of her temple at Deir el-Bahari, known to the ancient Egyptians as Djer-Djeseru, and dedicated to Hatshepsut's father Tuthmosis I and herself, as well as to Amun, United with Eternity. The temple took eight years to build and was constructed between the eighth and sixteenth years of her reign. She ruled from 1503 to 1452 B.C.

The scene begins with Amun-Re, King of the Gods, seated on his throne while the gods cluster around him. The text has been very much damaged, first by Tuthmosis III, when he built a temple next door and used Deir el-Bahari as a quarry, and then by Akhenaten who erased the name of Amun wherever it appeared.

Amun-Re looked at the gods and foretold the birth of Hatshepsut. He said, "I will create a queen to rule over Ta-mery (the Black Land of Egypt), I will unite the Two Lands in peace in her name, I will give her all lands and all countries." While he was speaking, Thoth, the vizier and messenger of the gods, entered. He reminded Amun-Re that in the palace of King Tuthmosis I was the Queen Ahmose, who alone could be the mother of the Great Queen. So Thoth and Amun-Re proceeded to the palace, Amun-Re in the guise of Ahmose's husband, Tuthmosis I. It was night and Queen Ahmose was asleep on her lion-headed couch.

The Queen awoke at the entry of the two gods, roused by the sweet perfumes that Amun-Re brought with him. Thinking she was with her husband, she sat with Amun-Re on a couch which was lifted from the earth and supported by two goddesses, so that their meeting should be neither on earth or in the sky. Amun-Re named his daughter to be, saying, "She shall be called Khemenet-Amun-Hatshepsut. She will exercise kingship over the whole land." Amun-Re then instructed the Creator God, Khnum, to form Hatshepsut on his potter's wheel, saying "For I will give her all life and satisfaction, all stability and all joy of heart forever."

Khnum at his potter's wheel

Khnum agreed to do this and said, "I will form your daughter, Makare Hatshepsut in Life, Prosperity and Health . . . her form will be more exalted than the gods, in her great dignity of the King of Upper and Lower Egypt." Khnum then took his potter's wheel and fashioned on it two children (they are shown as male children in the reliefs), Hatshepsut and her *Ka*.

The frog-headed goddess Heket, Goddess of Birth, kneels to the right and extends the *ankh*, the sign of life, to the children, so that they might live. Khnum then repeats his instructions and says he has carried them out and that Hatshepsut will appear as king upon the throne of Horus, like Re living forever. Five deities assist at the birth, Khnum, Heket of Heru, Isis, Nephthys, and Meskhenet, the Goddess presiding at Childbirth. Also in attendance were Taweret, the Goddess of Childbirth (in the form of a hippopotamus or a hippo-headed woman) and Bes (a dwarf god), the Protector of Children.

In due course Hatshepsut grew up and was crowned by her father Tuthmosis, as co-regent, before the assembled Egyptian court. This seems to have taken place not in Thebes but in Heliopolis and was a traditional act in connection with Egyptian kingship. Hatshepsut was enthroned in a duel ceremony, once before Atum, the most senior god, and once before Amun-Re, as King of the Gods. The new Great Queen is given her royal names and the crowns of Egypt. The records are kept by Sefkhet-Abwy and Thoth, accompanied by the words "Writing the name Golden Horus, Divine of Diadems: Writing the name King of Upper and Lower Egypt, Makare."

Thus all was ready that she should appear upon the throne of Horus before the glories of the Great House. And upon her was the favour of Amun-Re forever and ever.

The fragments of this story are to be found in the Harris Papyrus No. 500, discovered in 1874. The beginning of the story is lost but it strongly resembles later tales from the *Arabian Nights*. It dates to the Twentieth Dynasty B.C.

Once upon a time there was a general of the land of Egypt and his name was Thuthuti. He was one of the generals of the great Egyptian king Tuthmosis III who reigned between 1504-1450 B.C. And he followed the King on all his campaigns to the north and the south, and with him he crossed the great river Euphrates which runs upside down (the opposite way to the Nile) and he fought at the head of his soldiers, and he was rewarded by the King with the Gold of Valour. (This was a decoration in the form of gold flies given to anyone who distinguished themselves for outstanding bravery). And news arrived at the Egyptian court that the Prince of Joppa had revolted against the Egyptians, and he had killed the Egyptian soldiers and charioteers, murdered the governor and declared the town independent of Egypt. Now when the King heard what the messenger had to say he called together all his counsellors, nobles, wise men and scribes and told them of the message that he had received and asked their advice. Then Thuthuti rose up and said "O King on whom be Life, Health and Strength (the usual way of addressing an Egyptian ruler) command that I be given a troop of foot-soldiers of the Land of Egypt, and a battalion of charioteers, and I will bring the King of Joppa to account. But to help me in this difficult task I must be given the harpesh (sword) of the King, because without its help, I will not be able to overcome the enemy."

Harpesh

Then the King arose and said, "It is an excellent thing that you have said." And the great sword was given to him, and foot-soldiers and charioteers - even all he had asked for. Then he set out and after many days he arrived in the land of Djahy where Joppa was. He prepared to take the city, and he caused many sacks of skin to be made that would hold a man, and he prepared many fetters, and five hundred large jars of pottery, big enough to hold a man. Then he settled down outside the city of Joppa and prepared to take the city by his stratagem.

Thuthuti sent a message to the man of Joppa (the king) say-ing "I am Thuthuti, the general of the infantry of the land of Egypt, and I have followed his Majesty the King of Egypt, to the north, and the south, to the east and to the west, now the King of Egypt has become jealous of me, because of my many victories in his service, and I have escaped from Egypt with his great sword, and if you like I will give it to you, and also give you all the infan-try and charioteers of the land of Egypt that are with me, the flower of the brave ones of the army of Egypt." When the man of Joppa heard this, he knew that Thuthuti was one of the great ones of the land of Egypt, he had heard of his many victories, and he believed all that he said. So he told Thuthuti. "I will give you of the best of the land of Joppa if you give me the great sword of the King of Egypt, on whom be Life, Health and Strength." The man of Joppa came out of his city to the camp of Thuthuti, with his men, and when he came he asked to see the great sword of the

66

King of Egypt, he longed to possess it more than anything else because he thought that when he possessed it, he would be invincible, and would defeat his enemies. Now Thuthuti had hidden the sword among the sacks of forage of the chariot horses, so that the man of Joppa could not see it. Thuthuti had filled two of the large jars with treasure, and these he showed to the man of Joppa and said, "I have five hundred of these jars full of treasure and you can have them all, when I come to you." But the other four hundred and ninety-eight jars he had filled with the best of the soldiers of the land of Egypt, and the weapons of their bearers and he said, "Let us send these, as an earnest of my goodwill to you into your city." Five hundred of the soldiers of the land of Egypt were in the jars and one thousand of the soldiers were carrying them, two to each jar, and they entered straightaway into the city of Joppa by order of the King of Joppa. When they were within, the soldiers put down the jars, and out of them stepped the four hundred and ninety-eight soldiers, and they and the bearers of the jars fell on the guards of the gates and walls, and took the city of Joppa. They gave a great cry, and this was heard in the tents of the invading army, and the man of Joppa said "What is that?" Thuthuti said "It is my men taking the city of Joppa, and here", he said, "is the great sword of the King that you were so anxious to see." He drew it out of the bale of forage and smote the man of Joppa, who fell dead. And this is how Thuthuti, the general of the infantry of the land of Egypt took the city of Joppa. He sent a message to Egypt saying, "Rejoice, for I have taken the land of Joppa. Send then men to take these people to Egypt as captives, that you shall fill the house of Amun-Re, King of the Gods, with servants and slaves, and that the treasures of Joppa shall go to adorn his temples and your palaces."

This account was written down by the scribe, whose duty it was to write down the records of the victories of Egypt, and he wrote it all, and made a fair copy, and it has survived till this day, to tell the story of how Thuthuti the general of the King of Egypt, on whom be Life, Health and Strength, took the city of Joppa by a stratagem.

19   THE SPHINX AND THE KING'S DREAM

The account of this story is to be found in Breasted, *Ancient Records*, Vol. II, 810-815. It purported to be a royal inscription of the time of Tuthmosis IV of the Eighteenth Dynasty. However, mistakes in the text led Egyptologists to suppose that it is a later copy. It was found on a large granite slab lying between the paws of the sphinx, uncovered by Caviglia in 1818.

Once upon a time there was a king called Tuthmosis; he was not the great king of that name who had ruled Egypt, but his grandson. As a young man he was devoted to all kinds of field sports, particularly hunting. He was also good at target practise, shooting at the target with copper bolts while driving past in his chariot. He also loved hunting in the desert, especially in the Valley of the Gazelles near Memphis, which was well-known for its large quantity of game. One day, when he was out hunting in the Valley, accompanied by a few followers, the time came for the midday siesta. He was near the sphinx, which in those days was covered by sand right up to its ears, and while he rested in its shade he fell asleep.

Re-Harakhti

68

The sphinx represented a Sun God called Harakhte meaning "Horus of the Horizon", which referred to the god rising at dawn to bathe in "the field of rushes". Anyway, while Tuthmosis was asleep, he had a dream in which Harakhte appeared to him and asked him to clear away the sand which was covering him and encroaching on him more and more each day. He told Tuthmosis that if he did so he would become King of Egypt. Tuthmosis was surprised because at this time he was a younger son not strictly in line of succession. When he woke up, he ordered offerings to be made to the god, and had all the sand cleared away from the sphinx. In due course, Tuthmosis did become King of Egypt and reigned for eight years.

This text was adapted from *Les Contes Populaires de l'Egypte Ancienne*. Another version in the form of a folk tale was told to John Pendlebury when he was working at el-Amarna in 1939 but this related to the young sheikh of el Til and not the Prince of Egypt.

Once upon a time there was a king and queen of Egypt and they had no children, so they prayed to the gods to send them a child, and the gods favoured them and in due course a son was born to them. To the naming of the prince came the Seven Hathors which are the Seven Fates in Egypt and they looked at the young child and they said, "He will die by the snake, or by the crocodile or by the dog", and they went away. The king and queen were very upset and to prevent this happening they built a high tower and shut up the young prince in this, with first his nurse and later his tutor. One day, when he was a youth, he was looking out of the window when he saw a puppy playing on the bank of the river, and he asked his tutor what this was, and he told him it was a puppy. Then the young prince said he would like to have one, but it was explained to him that he could not, because it was his fate to die by the dog, or by the crocodile or by the snake. But you know how it is. The prince had set his mind on it, and when a prince wants something he is bound to get it in the end, and he made such a fuss that eventually they got him a dog. Meanwhile, although he was confined and could not go out freely in the countryside, he had been trained to ride a horse, and to shoot with the bow and arrow, and strike with the harpesh, the royal weapon rather like a curved sword. One day when he was visited by his parents, he told them that he was tired of staying cooped up in a tower, and that he would rather go out and meet his fate. Naturally they argued with him, but it was very little use; he had set his mind on trying his luck in the outside world. In the end they gave in and allowed him to go, so that he set out on his horse followed by his faithful dog.

He went through Egypt and from Egypt to Sinai, Palestine and Syria. When he arrived at Naharain, which was part of Syria bordering on the Euphrates, he went to the capital, and found that it was in a state of great excitement. This was because the King of Naharain had promised his beautiful daughter to the first prince

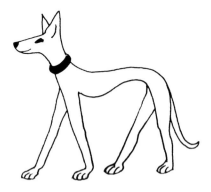

Saluki dog

who could scale the outside of the citadel and reach her chamber. Naturally all the young Syrian princes were eager to try, and when the young Egyptian prince arrived they were making preparations to climb the formidable citadel. Now although he had not told his parents, the young Egyptian prince had been in the habit of climbing in and out of his tower since he was a small boy, just to show that he could, so that climbing up the outside of the citadel, presented for him few problems. He started to climb, and in a short while arrived at the princess's window, and she helped him inside. The king came hurrying up and said, "Now which of the princes are you?" For some reason, not entirely clear to us, perhaps he feared that Egypt and Naharain were not on good terms, the young prince replied that he was the son of the chief of the charioteers of the King of Egypt. The king was furious and said to his daughter, "You must choose a proper prince, this is only a charioteer, we will reward him and send him away." But the princess replied, "No, I like him better than the other princes, and if I cannot marry him, I will not marry any of the others." Well, you know how it is! It is no use arguing with a princess any more than it is of use arguing with a prince, and the king finally had to give way. So that they got married and set off to return to Egypt.

While they were crossing the Great Syrian Desert, they had to stop for the night, and the Prince who was very tired went heavily to sleep. Luckily the princess awoke at the sound of a rustling in the tent, and saw a large snake gliding towards her husband. She hurriedly poured out a bowl of milk and put it in the snake's path. Well, you know how fond snakes are of milk, so that it drank it all and then fell fast asleep. So that the princess who had been watching all this, took her husband's sword and cut off the snake's head. Thus he escaped the first of his three fates.

When they got back to Egypt, the first thing that the prince could think of doing, all tired and dirty, was to swim in the Nile, but as soon as he had plunged in, the largest crocodile you ever saw surfaced near him and said, "You cannot escape me for I am your fate! There is only one means of escaping me and that is if you can dig a hole in the sand, which will remain full of water, and then my spell will be broken. If not death will come to you speedily, for you cannot escape." When the young man heard these words he was full of gloom, and he returned to the palace and shut himself up in his room, refusing to speak even to the princess. However, by evening she had managed to penetrate his room and find out what was the matter. "How can a hole in the sand remain full of water, the crocodile might as well have killed me at once, as there is no chance of my being able to break his spell", said the prince. The princess was a girl of infinite ingenuity, so she said, "Is that all. I can deal with that, for I had a fairy godmother who taught me the uses of many plants, and I know that not far from here in the desert, grows a small plant with four leaves, that will keep the water in the pit for a whole year. You just start digging holes, and filling them with water to keep the crocodile happy, and as soon as it is dawn I will set out on my donkey to look for the right herb." Now the princess had a splendid white donkey, and on this she set out into the Western Desert, even before it was light. At first she could only see the flat sandy desert, but soon she saw a high hill with a rock sticking out of it, which was what she was looking for. She stopped in the shade of the hill, and with

72

great difficulty and the aid of a rope that she had brought, she climbed the hill. When she got to the top a strong wind was blowing, and this blew all the sand and grit into her face, so that she could not see what she was doing. She had to grope about with her hands, and at first she thought that there was nothing there. Finally, however, she found the plant stuck in a crevice of rock, and was able to count that it had four leaves. She then set out down the hill again, got back to the donkey, and set off again across the desert to return to the prince.

The prince was by this time quite exhausted; he had been digging holes in the sand all day. He was not used to such work and every time he filled the holes in the sand with water, it ran out, and the crocodile was there with his jaws open, saying things like, "Faster, faster" or "I am getting quite hungry watching you work" or "I do not suppose your wife will be back before I eat you" and other cheering remarks. When the princess arrived he had just dug a particularly fine hole, so that he was able to pour in the water from a large water-jar right away, and when the water reached the top, the princess flung in the four-leaved plant. They were then in a very anxious state in case the water did not remain in the hole. But after half an hour it was still as full as before, and the crocodile had sulkily to admit defeat and went away. Thus the prince escaped the second of his three fates.

The prince and princess were staying at Memphis, when they heard that the old king who was living at Thebes had fallen ill. They became anxious to see him, so they set off in the royal *dahabiyah* (sailing boat) to see him. However, it was the time of the low Nile, when the river was very shallow, and as they came round the bend from Dendera, where the river makes a great loop, the boat ran on a sand bank and the crew could not get it off, added to this the north wind, which usually blew steadily enabling them to sail up stream against the current, died away. So the prince and princess got off the boat and decided to go overland across the desert to Thebes. They did so, but it took them rather longer than they expected, and when night came they had to take refuge in a cave. During the night a band of robbers passed by, their dog barked at them and the robbers rushed in and killed both the prince and princess. Thus he finally met his third fate, which he could not escape.

This tale which is one of the best known Egyptian stories, exists only in one papyrus, that of Madame d'Orbiney bought by the British Museum in 1857. The papyrus is Nineteenth Dynasty in date, and is known to have been in the possession of Sety II when he was heir to the throne. It is likely that it embodies earlier elements. It has had many translations, and probably dates originally to the early part of the Eighteenth Dynasty.

Once upon a time there were two brothers, Anpu was the name of the elder and Bata was the name of the younger. Now their parents were dead, and the elder brother stood as it were as a father to his younger brother. The boy lived in his house and Anpu provided him with everything, food, clothes and shelter. As a result Bata worked well and willingly for his brother. It was he who did the hoeing, and who took out the animals to the fields. Now the spirit of the gods was in Bata, and there was not his equal in the whole land. He took out the cattle daily and they told him where the best pasture was to be found. He listened to them, for he understood the language of animals. As a result the animals that he looked after were always in a good state, and increased in number. He worked from early morning to evening, and his brother respected his work. But the wife of his brother was jealous of the youth and thought that her husband paid too much attention to him instead of to her, so that one day when Bata was sent back by his brother to collect a load of corn for sowing and she was busy doing her hair, she refused to help him lift the heavy load on his shoulder, some five bushels, and then pretended to her husband when he came home ahead of Bata, that the latter had attacked her. She did not prepare the evening meal and sat in the dust with her face streaked with tears and her clothes torn. Naturally Anpu believed what she said, and in a fury he waited behind the stable

74

door to kill Bata with an axe as he entered. As the animals went into the stable with Bata driving them, the first cow said to Bata, "Look, your brother Anpu is standing behind the door with an axe ready to kill you." The second said the same, and when Bata looked under the door there were his brother's feet. So Bata fled and his brother followed him, but the gods protected Bata, and they placed a canal filled with crocodiles between the two brothers and Anpu was afraid to cross it.

Bata called upon Re-Harakhte, the Sun God, to hear him and to judge between them. When the sun rose Bata told his brother that he was blameless, but because Anpu had not trusted him he would go away and leave him and live in the Valley of the Acacias. Bata to protect himself placed his *Ba* (soul) in the top of an acacia tree and said that if anything happened to him, Anpu would know because his evening beer would turn muddy and he was to come and look for him, and when he found Bata's soul, he was to place it in a cup of water, so that he could live again and tell him everything that had happened to him.

So Bata went away to the Valley of the Acacias, and he was alone, and he spent his time hunting in the desert. He built himself a house, that he might have somewhere to live. And the Nine Gods went through the Land of Egypt, and they saw that Bata was alone and Re-Harakhte said to Khnum, the Fashioner of Men, who makes mankind on his potter's wheel, "Look, Bata is all alone. Let us send someone to keep him company." And Khnum fashioned a woman on his wheel, and she was more beautiful than anyone, but when the Seven Hathors that foretell the fate of men saw her, they said, "She will die a sharp death." For though Khnum had fashioned a beautiful woman he had omitted to give her a good heart.

Everyday Bata went hunting to provide food for her, and he loved her very much, but he was afraid that Hapi, the God of the Nile Inundation, would see her and snatch her from him. So he said to the woman "Do not go outside for fear of the river", but she took no notice, and walked by the side of the river, and Hapi saw her and desired her, and sent his waves up the bank to catch her, but she escaped and he only tore off a lock of her hair. Now this hair was scented with all sweet perfumes because she was made of the essence of the gods, and it floated down the river till it got to the place where the king's washer-women were washing the royal clothes. The chief fuller found the lock of hair, and because it was sweetly perfumed and made all the clothes smell sweet, he took it to the king. The people spoke and said the woman from whom this hair came must be the daughter of the gods, perhaps even the daughter of Re-Harakhte himself. The king was moved by a desire to see the woman from whom the lock of hair had come, so he sent out messengers to every quarter of the country to enquire for her, and they all returned except those who had been sent to the Valley of the Acacias and these did not return, because Bata had killed everyone of them. So His Majesty, on whom be Life, Health and Strength, sent many men and soldiers, and they killed Bata, and took the girl back to the king. And the king was delighted with her, and took her into the palace and made her one of his wives.

Now Bata's brother, Anpu, went into his house one evening to have his cup of beer, and when he looked at it, it was cloudy and troubled. Then he knew that something had happened to Bata. So he went to the Valley of the Acacias and entered Bata's house, and he found him lying dead upon his mat. Then he set to work to find Bata's soul, and he looked for it for three days, and on the morning of the fourth day, just when the sun had risen, he found it. Then he took a cup of water and placed the soul in it, and when it had sucked up all the water, Bata shivered in all his limbs and he looked at his brother, and he told him all that had happened. And then Bata said to his elder brother, "Look I am going to turn into a great black bull, with every good mark, and you will take me to the king, so that I may return a rough answer to my wife." Then Bata turned into a great black bull, and Anpu rode on his back, until they came to the place where the court was. The king was delighted, and he paid Anpu much gold and silver, and he returned to his village. The king made offerings to the bull and was very pleased with it. And one day when the girl who had been his wife came to the purified place, the bull spoke to her and he said, "Behold I am alive!" and she said, "Who are you?" And he replied "I am Bata." And she was very alarmed, and she cast about for a way to destroy him. Then she pleased the king, and he prom-

76

ised her that he would do anything that she asked. So she asked for the liver of the bull roasted. Now the king was exceedingly sad, but he had promised the girl, so ordered a great feast to be made for the bull, and many offerings were brought, and at the end of the day the king caused the bull to be sacrificed. As they were doing this he shook his head, and two drops of blood fell one each side of the door of the House of the King and from this blood sprouted up two beautiful Persea trees. And this was reported to the king who was very pleased, and he rode in his chariot to see this wonder, and his queen went with him, and when they drew up beneath the Persea trees, the trees spoke to her and said, "O you deceitful one, I am Bata, I am alive, though I have been badly treated. It is you who had me destroyed, who had the acacia tree where my soul was, cut down, who caused the bull which I had become to be killed."

The great bull

And the queen was very upset, and she set her mind to please the king again, and again she persuaded him to do anything that she said. Then she asked that the two Persea trees should be cut down, and the wood made into planks. All was done as she had directed, and she stood by to see that it was done. While she was watching, a chip of wood flew from the tree into her mouth and she swallowed it. In due course she bore the king a son, and as a result there were rejoicings in the whole land. And the king was very pleased and made him the Royal son, Viceroy of Kush. Now after many days when the king had fulfilled his life, he flew up to heaven leaving a Horus in his place. This was the young prince. When the young prince had become king, he sent for his chief ministers and said, "Let the chief of my ministers be brought, so that they shall know what has happened to me. For know that I am Bata, that this woman my mother and my wife has tried to destroy me three times, but each time I have escaped her." They judged her and she was taken out into the desert and torn to pieces by being tied to the tails of wild horses. But Anpu was brought to court, and made a great noble, and when Bata died in due course, it was his brother who saw to everything on his day of burial, and in due course Anpu sat on the throne of the Land of Egypt.

Excellently finished for the soul of the scribe Kagabu of the Treasury of the King, and for the scribe Hora, and for the scribe Anena, the owner of this roll. He who speaks against this roll, may Thoth destroy him.

22   THE PRINCESS OF BEKHTEN

This text comes from a stele once said to have been found in the temple of Khonsu-Neferhotep at Karnak by François Champollion, but now thought to have been found in a small Ptolemaic sanctuary near the temple of Khonsu, and moved to Paris in 1846 by Prisse d'Avenne, by whom it was given to the Bibliothèque Nationale of Paris. Set in the Nineteenth Dynasty reputedly under Ramesses II, it is in reality a later forgery, written to enhance the position of Khonsu by his priests probably during the Twenty-Sixth Dynasty.

It was in the reign of King Ramesses II, son of the Sun, be-loved of Amun, King of the Gods. A great king, and a great warrior was Ramesses, like Montu in the day of battle, very brave he was and very strong. One day the king was in Naharain, where the great River Euphrates rolls down to the sea. Here he was receiving the tribute of the vassal princes of Asia, for he was the conqueror of the Nine Archer tribes. No one could stand before him when he went to war. All the princes bowed before him, and they brought him gold, and precious stones, and sweetly scented woods, and slaves and cattle. And the Prince of Bekhten came too and brought his eldest daughter, very beautiful she was, like a slender palm tree. And the king was delighted with her and decided to marry her, and he gave her an Egyptian name, Nefru-Re, so that she should be known by it throughout the Land of Egypt. Then King Ramesses returned to Egypt, after he had received all the tribute, and with him went his new wife, Nefru-Re.

On the twenty-second day of the month of Payni, King Ramesses went to the Temple of Amun, because it was the very beautiful festival of the god, when the Sacred Boat is taken out with the figure of Amun in it, so that all may see him and wonder. Then there came to the temple some of the courtiers to say that messengers had arrived from the Prince of Bekhten, to say that the small sister of Nefru-Re had fallen ill, and the Prince of Bekhten wanted the Egyptian king to send one of his wise men to cure the princess. Messengers were sent to the "House of Life" and they sent Tehuti-em-heb, a scribe and doctor learned and skilled in his profession, to cure the Princess Bentreshy. But when he got to Naharain, he found that the princess was possessed of a demon, a spirit that was hostile to him, and against whom all his skill was of no avail. Then Tehuti-em-heb counselled the Prince of Bekhten to send again to Egypt for a god to fight against this spirit. So the Prince of Bekhten sent again to Egypt, and his messenger arrived in year twenty-six, the first month of summer while the king was again celebrating the Feast of Amun at Thebes. And His Majesty reported to Khonsu-Neferhotep in Thebes and asked for his help. And Khonsu-Neferhotep sent for Khonsu, Expeller of Demons, who is also called Khonsu, the Provider and the Protector. Khonsu-Neferhotep assented to Khonsu, Expeller of Demons being sent to Bekhten, and he made a special protection for him.

Now the distance from Bekhten to Egypt was so great that it took three years to make the journey, and throughout this time the evil spirit lived in Bentreshy and would not leave her. When the preparations had been made, Khonsu, the Expeller of Demons left for Bekhten. His retinue was that of a king for he was greatly honoured by the Egyptian people. This time they made rather better time and arrived at Bekhten after one year and five months.

The Prince of Bekhten came out to greet Khonsu, Expeller of Demons, with all his retinue. He was brought into the chamber of Bentreshy, the little sister of the Royal Wife. He made a magical protection over her and in a moment she was well. Then the spirit who was in her spoke to Khonsu, Expeller of Demons, "You have come in peace, O Great God, Expeller of Demons. Bekhten is your city, its people are your slaves. I bow before you for I am also your slave. I will go from this place, to where I came from, so that your heart may have peace. But before I go, order that a Holy Day be made for me by the Prince of Bekhten." When he heard these words Khonsu inclined his head to the spirit and said, "Let the Prince of Bekhten make a great sacrifice for this spirit."

At this marvellous act, the Prince of Bekhten, and the people of Bekhten were very much afraid, and they prepared a great sacrifice for the spirit. Then the spirit in the form of a "Shining One"

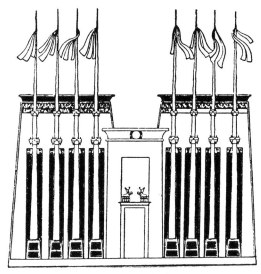

The Temple of Khonsu

went in peace from the Land of Bekhten. The Prince of Bekhten was pleased, but he was afraid that the spirit might return and again take up residence in Bentreshy, or somewhere else. So instead of sending back Khonsu, Expeller of Demons, he kept him in his palace. And the god stayed for three years, four months and five days in Bekhten.

Then one night when the Prince of Bekhten was asleep, he dreamed that he saw Khonsu in the form of a great hawk of gold leave his statue and set his course to fly back to Egypt. Then he knew that it was no use holding on to the statue of the god as its soul had departed, and he said, "This god who has dwelt with us, he desires to return to Egypt. Let his chariot also be sent with him." And the Prince of Bekhten ordered that everything should be prepared for the journey, and he gave many presents to the god, and he arranged for a strong bodyguard of many soldiers and many chariots, so that the god should return in state to his own country.

When they arrived in Thebes after a journey of many months, Khonsu, Expeller of Demons, gave all that he had received from the Prince of Bekhten to Khonsu-Neferhotep, and he returned to his temple in peace, and all this took place in the reign of His Majesty on whom be Life, Health and Strength, Ramesses living for ever.

23   SATNI-KHAMOSE AND THE MUMMIES

Several versions of the papyrus on which this story is based exist. They are to be found in the Cairo Museum, and date to a late period, probably Ptolemaic, that is between 330-30 B.C. The name of the king in whose reign they were written down has not survived. It was published first by Mariette in 1871 in *Les Papyrus du Musée du Boulaq* and by Brugsch a little earlier in 1867 in the *Revue Archéologique,* vol. XVI. It was later worked over by Petrie in *Egyptian Tales,* 1895, F. Griffith, *Stories of the High Priests of Memphis,* 1900, and Gaston Maspero, *Stories of Ancient Egypt,* 1915.

Once upon a time there was a king of ancient Egypt called Usermare Ramesses II and he reigned from 1304 to 1237 B.C. and he had many sons. One of these was called Satni-Khamose and he was a very learned man, and used to spend his whole time wandering about the temples and studying the sacred writings that were to be found in the temple libraries. One day as he was going round the temple of Ptah at Memphis reading the inscriptions on the walls, he was approached by a priest, who laughed at him and said, "Why do you waste your time studying these writings which will not bring you any power. Come with me and I will show you the place where the Book of Thoth is." Now Thoth was the God of Wisdom, and he had a book wherein was written all that was then known in the world, and anyone who read it could enchant the sea, and enchant the sky, and understand all that the birds said, and the animals, and could control everything by his magic power. But the priest said to Satni-Khamose, "This book is in the tomb of Nefer-ka-Ptah, and he will not yield it to you easily, in fact if you take it from him, he will make you bring it back to him with a forked stick, and a staff in your hand and a lighted brazier on your head."

From the moment that he heard these words Satni-Khamose had no more peace of mind. He could not settle to anything, and did not know in what part of the world he was. So that he went to the king and explained his case and asked permission to go down to the cemetery at Saqqara where Nefer-ka-Ptah was buried and bring back the Book of Thoth. So he went to the necropolis of Memphis, that is Saqqara, with his foster brother Ankh-Horus, and after searching for three days they found the tomb chapel, by reading the stele with Nefer-ka-Ptah's name and titles.

Now Satni was already a magician so that when he found the tomb he recited a spell and the earth opened in front of him and he went down into the burial chamber, which was as bright as day, because of the light shed by the Book of Thoth. And in the tomb he found Nefer-ka-Ptah and his wife Ahura and their son Merab. Now though it was really the mummy of Nefer-ka-Ptah, those of Ahura and Merab were only doubles, or *Kas* because they were not

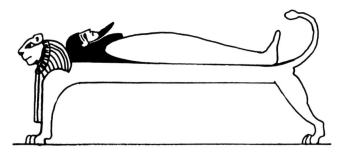

Mummy on a bier

buried here but at Coptos. That is why the priest who was really Nefer-ka-Ptah had appeared to Satni-Khamose in the temple, because he wanted the bodies of his wife and son brought from Coptos to be placed in the tomb with him, so that they could all be together.

Now Ahura tried to discourage Satni-Khamose from taking the Book of Thoth, and she told him the terrible fate that had befallen them as a result of taking the Book. The beginning of her story was very like that which had happened to Satni-Khamose already. Nefer-ka-Ptah had also enjoyed studying the learned writings and going round the temples reading the inscriptions and like Satni-Khamose, he also was a son of a king of Egypt, but of an earlier day.

Again he too was approached by a priest who laughed at him, and told him he was wasting his time when he should be looking for the Book of Thoth, by whose means he could enchant the sky, and enchant the earth, and understand what the animals and the birds were saying and everything that was going on in the world. The priest told Nefer-ka-Ptah that he would tell him where the Book was to be found if he would pay for a good burial for him, and have a splendid coffin made for his body. Now Nefer-ka-Ptah arranged all that; and then he called upon the priest to tell him where the Book of Thoth was to be found. So the priest said, "The Book of Thoth is to be found in the river of Coptos (that is part of the Nile that flows in the district of Coptos, a town in Upper Egypt). It is in an iron coffer, and the iron coffer is over a bronze coffer, and the bronze coffer is over a box of cinnamon wood, and the box of cinnamon wood is over a box of ivory, and the box of ivory is over a box of ebony, and inside the box of ebony is a silver box and inside the silver box is a gold box, and inside this is the Book of Thoth. And these boxes are guarded by all kinds of snakes and reptiles and round the iron box is coiled the snake that no-man-can-kill." From the time that the priest spoke to Nefer-ka-Ptah he lost interest in everything else, and he did not know in what part of the world he was. He came out of the temple, he went home and told Ahura all that had happened to him. She became very alarmed, for she saw that no good would come of this, and tried to persuade Nefer-ka-Ptah to forget all about it. But no, he went to his father the king, on whom be Life, Health and Strength, and asked him if he could borrow the royal barge to go up river to Coptos. The king of course agreed, and Nefer-ka-Ptah, Ahura and Merab, their son, set out in the royal boat to go to Coptos. When they arrived at Coptos they were made welcome by the priests of Isis and Horus. Nefer-ka-Ptah caused a bull to be brought, and a goose and he made an offering and poured a libation of wine to the two gods so that events should be favourable. Then he collected a lot of beeswax and fashioned a magic boat,

84

and filled it with models of sailors and recited a spell over it to bring them to life, and when he had done so, he placed the boat in the river, and said to the sailors, "Row for me, row for me." And they did and in three days the magic boat had brought him to where the chest was at the bottom of the river. But Ahura and the boy Merab had remained behind at Coptos, and all the time Ahura had cried and lamented because she was afraid of what would happen to her husband.

Now when Nefer-ka-Ptah had arrived at the place where the chest was, he contrived by means of his magic to make the water of the river rise up on each side like a wall, leaving the bed of the stream clear. Then he saw the chest, and it was surrounded by snakes and scorpions. By his magic power, he was able to enchant all these so that they fell into a deep sleep, all except the snake that no-man-can-kill, who arose and hissed at him. Then he took his sword and cut off its head, but it immediately came to life again, and where one head had been there were now two, and he cut it off again, but the same thing happened, only now three heads appeared. He was in despair when he thought to sprinkle sand on the stump, and however hard it tried the snake could not get his head fixed on firmly again. So that Nefer-ka-Ptah could finally turn his attention to the chest in which was the Book of Thoth. He saw that it was an iron coffer, and he opened it and found inside it a bronze coffer, inside this was a cinnamon wood box, inside this was a box of ivory, and inside this was an ebony box, inside this was a silver box and inside this was a box of gold in which was the Book of Thoth. When Nefer-ka-Ptah drew out the book he recited a formula of what was written in it. He enchanted the heavens, he enchanted the sky, he enchanted the earth, he understood what the birds said, and the animals and the fishes in the river, and the seas. He saw the sun as it mounted in the sky, with its cycle of the gods, and the moon and the stars. And he took the book, and he returned to the wax boat, and he said to the sailors, "Row for me, row for me, take me back to Coptos." And they did, and he returned to where Ahura and the boy Merab waited for him. And Ahura had sat silently waiting for him, not eating or sleeping till he returned. And she put out her hand and took the Book of Thoth and she too enchanted the heavens and the earth, and heard what the birds, and animals and fishes said, and saw the sun rising, and the moon in the sky and the cycle of the gods. And Nefer-ka-Ptah took ink and he wrote all that was in the Book, and he took beer and washed away the writing, and he drank it, and he knew forever all that was written in the Book of Thoth.

Then Nefer-ka-Ptah and Ahura made offerings for his safe return, and after the requisite time had passed, they embarked on the royal barge and set out for Memphis. Now Thoth was furious when he found out what had happened to his book. And he went up to Re, the king of the gods, and he pleaded with him to let him have Nefer-ka-Ptah, who had stolen his book from him. And Re said to him, "He is all yours, do with him what you will." And at that moment the royal barge was sailing northwards towards Memphis, and the boy Merab came out from under the awning, and by the power of Thoth he was drawn over the side and drowned.

Nefer-ka-Ptah by the power of the Book was able to hear from the boy what had happened, and how Re had given him over to Thoth for vengeance. Then they turned round the royal barge, because the souls of men cannot rest till the right burial rites are carried out, and they took the boy's body back to Coptos, and they built a tomb, and had the body embalmed, and all this took seventy-two days, and when the funeral was over and the body laid to rest, they set off again for Memphis. And when they arrived at the same spot on the river where the boy had met his death, the power of Thoth drew Ahura out from under the awning, and she fell in the river and was drowned. So Nefer-ka-Ptah by his magic means brought up her body also, and heard what had happened, and turned round the royal barge and went back to Coptos, where after she was embalmed, she was buried in the same tomb as her son. But Nefer-ka-Ptah returned to the royal barge and set sail again for Memphis. He knew that he could not escape his fate, but he tied to his waist the Book of Thoth, so that even if he died, Thoth should not have it. When the boat reached the same place, the power of Thoth drew him out from under the awning and he fell in the river and was drowned, but by the power of the Book, his body became entangled with the steering ropes and it was dragged behind the royal barge all the way to Memphis. Here it was found, taken out and buried with all the appropriate rites in the burial ground of Memphis at Saqqara.

However, Satni-Khamose was unmoved by all this tale of woe and when Ahura had finished her story all he said was "Give me the Book of Thoth. If you will not give it to me I will take it by force." Nefer-ka-Ptah then raised himself up on his bier and said, "Are you capable of obtaining this Book by your power as an excellent scribe, or by skill in playing against me? Let us play for it." Satni agreed to this proposal, and the gameboard was produced and the dogs that were on it, and they played. Nefer-ka-Ptah won a game from Satni, and Nefer-ka-Ptah caused Satni to sink into the earth up to his legs. They played a second time, and again Satni lost, and this time he sank up to his waist, and with a third game Satni sank into the ground up to his armpits. Then he called on his foster-brother to help him and to bring him his books of magic and his talismans to protect him, and with their help he got out of this difficulty. When Satni rose from the earth, he stretched out his hand and took the Book of Thoth from where it lay between Nefer-ka-Ptah and Ahura, and as he went out of the tomb, darkness descended behind him, because the only light was that of the Book. Then said Nefer-ka-Ptah to Ahura, "Do not be distressed because of this, I will make him bring it back with a forked stick in his hand, and a lighted brazier on his head."

Satni, when he came out, told the king all that had happened to him, and he was advised to return the Book to Nefer-ka-Ptah, but he would not, and instead spent all his time reading it. Everything then went wrong for him. He ceased to pay attention to his affairs because of the Book, he fell in love with a priestess who took all his possessions from him, he lost his wife, his children died, and his house was burnt down. All these were punishments sent to him because he had taken something which was not his. He finally found himself outside the city walls without a rag to his back, and was forced to go to the king and admit he had made a mistake. The king then advised him to take a forked stick in his hand and a lighted brazier on his head, and to go back to the tomb and restore the Book to Nefer-ka-Ptah. So this is what Satni did. When he got to the tomb he restored the brightness to it which had been missing when he took the book away. Then Nefer-ka-

Ptah said to him, "There is one more thing that you must do before we can rest in peace. You must go to Coptos, and find where
Ahura and Merab were buried, and you must bring their bodies
here so that we can all rest in one tomb." So Satni went to the
king his father, on whom be Life, Health and Strength, and asked
for the royal barge to take him up to Coptos. There he spent three
days and nights searching for the place of rest of Ahura and the
boy Merab and finally he was helped by an old man who told him
that the tomb was under the corner of the priest's house. There he
found the tomb and the mummies. He took them and brought
them by water to Saqqara, where they were placed in the tomb
with Nefer-ka-Ptah and the Book of Thoth.

This complete writing where is related the story of Satni-
Khamose and Nefer-ka-Ptah, was written by the scribe Zihharpto,
in year 35 in the month of Tybi.

24   SATNI-KHAMOSE AND THE AFTERWORLD

This story is preserved in a Ptolemaic papyrus now in the Cairo Museum (No. 30646).

The story goes that when Satni-Khamose was a small boy, he lived with his father in a house in Thebes which overlooked the West Gate of the city through which the burials, taken to the West Bank, went. One day when they were looking out, Satni-Khamose and his father saw two funerals passing by. One was that of a rich man with mourners and many offerings and offering bearers, the other was that of a poor man who had no one following him and who was wrapped in his single garment and tied onto the back of an ass. When Satni-Khamose and his father saw this, his father said to Khamose, "I hope that when I die my funeral will be like that of the rich man." But Satni said to his father, "No father, it would be much better if your funeral was that of the poor man." Then because Satni-Khamose was already a magician, even though he was a small boy of about twelve years of age, he took his father by the hand and drew him to Abydos, north of Thebes, where there was the entry to the Afterworld through a gap in the hills to the west of the cemetery.

Judgement scene

89

They entered the Afterworld and proceeded through five of the divisions until they reached the sixth division where the Hall of Judgement was, and Osiris was there judging the quick and the dead. The gate to this division was turning in its socket and in the socket was a man who was crying aloud with the pain of the gate turning upon him. Satni-Khamose turned to his father and said, "This is the rich man whose funeral you saw a short time ago." Then Satni-Khamose pointed to a figure dressed all in shining white who was standing behind the throne of Osiris and said to his father, "Father this is the poor man whose funeral you saw this morning in Thebes."

25   SATNI-KHAMOSE AND THE MAGICIAN

This story is a late story probably of Ptolemaic date.

The story goes that the King of Ethiopia wished to prove that he and his magicians were stronger and more efficient than those of the ancient Egyptians. So that he sent to the Egyptian Court his most expert magician, a tall Ethiopian over seven feet in height. And he came to the Egyptian court at Memphis, and he challenged the Egyptian magicians to feats of magic. First he performed some magic and removed the King of Egypt from his palace during the night and beat him with many blows, so that in the morning he

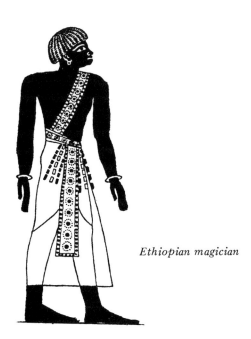

Ethiopian magician

was battered and bruised. Then the Egyptian king called on his magicians to retaliate. Now Satni-Khamose was not yet grown up, and his father was one of the chief wise men and magicians of the court, but he already knew that his son was to be a greater man than he was. So he said to the king and the Ethiopian magician, "This is such a small magic that you have made that I will call my son who is yet a youth to reply to you." Then Satni-Khamose performed magic and he caused the King of Ethiopia to be taken from his palace and beaten during the night. But to prevent retaliation he made a very strong magic to prevent the Ethiopian from removing the King of Egypt from his palace again.

26 THE JOURNEY OF WEN-AMUN TO THE SYRIAN COAST

The text on which this story is based was found at el-Hibeh near al-Fashn in the autumn of 1891. It was incomplete and passed into the hands of Golenischeff, who in 1898 prepared a Russian translation accompanied by a phototype of the first 21 lines in the *Recueil de Mémoires* presented to M. de Rosen by his pupils of the University of Petrograd (now Leningrad) on the occasion of his jubilee. Further fragments were found by one of the Antiquities Inspectors, Henri Brugsch in 1892 in a collection of papyri which he had acquired. It has been translated into several languages, and it is still uncertain whether it is a report of an actual official journey or a literary work of the Late Period. It is dated to the eleventh century B.C.

Year 5, fourth month of the Third Season, day 16. The day on which the Elder of the Gate of the Temple of Amun (*Ipetisut*) Lord of the Two Lands Wen-Amun departed from Thebes in order to obtain wood for the boat of Amun-Re, King of the Gods,

The boat of Amun

whose name (the boat's) is "Amun strong of Leadership". The day I arrived at Tanis (a city in the Delta) at the place where Smendes and Tanet-Amun were, I gave them the dispatches of Amun-Re, King of the Gods, and they had them read before them, and they said, "Let it be done as Amun-Re, Lord of the Gods has ordered."

I remained until the fourth month of the Harvest in Tanis, and then Smendes and Tenet-Amun sent me with the ship's captain Mangabuti, and I embarked with him on the great green Syrian Sea, on the first day of the fourth month of the Harvest.

Within a month I had reached the city of Dor, a port south of Mount Carmel on the Palestinian coast, a city of the Tjeker. The chief of Dor, called Badr or Badilu, sent to Wen-Amun provisions in the shape of ten thousand loaves of bread, a flask of wine, and a haunch of beef. While they were in the port one of the crew deserted, and took with him goods of Wen-Amun: vessels of gold worth 5 deben, five jars of silver worth 20 deben, and a small bag containing 11 deben of silver which made a total of 5 deben of gold and 31 deben of silver (1 deben = 91 grams.). And I Wen-Amun arose early in the morning and I went to the ruler of the port, and I said, "I have been robbed in your port. Now it is you who are the ruler of this country, who are its judge and administrator, look for my gold for me. For this gold, it belongs not to me but to Amun-Re, King of the Gods, Lord of all the Countries, and it belongs to Smendes, Ruler of Tanis and to Herihor, my master, and to the other nobles of Egypt, and it also belongs to Zikar-Baal, Lord of Byblos."

And he said to me, "O, Excellency, be not annoyed. I know nothing of this tale that you tell me. If the thief is one of my country, I will return it from my treasury. But I do not know who he is, so wait here several days while a search is being made for him." So I waited for nine days in the port of Dor. At the end of this time I went to the Prince and said, "You have not found my silver, I will arise and go with the captain of the ship to Tyre, and if you find my money, keep it, and I will call back on my way back to Egypt and if you have found it I will collect it from you."

And on the 20th day of the fourth month of Harvest I embarked again on the Great Syrian Sea and I went to Tyre and I complained to the ruler of Tyre of the behaviour of the Prince of

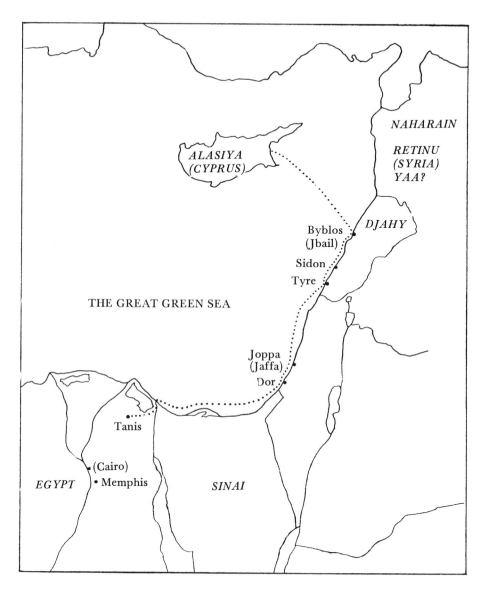

Sketch map of the Journey of Wen-amun

95

Dor. But he of Tyre was a friend of the Prince of Dor and he said to me, "Be silent, or a misfortune will happen to you."

And I arose and I departed next morning from Tyre to go to Byblos, and when we arrived at the port of Byblos I searched the vessel and found that on board were some men of Tjeker, and I searched their things, and I took from them 30 deben of silver, and I said to them, "Look I have taken your silver, and it will remain with me, until you find the money which was stolen from me." And I disembarked and I took the travelling statue of Amun-Re, Lord of the Ways, in its shrine, and I placed inside it the equipment of the god. And the Prince of Byblos sent to me and said, "Depart from my port." And I explained that I had only taken goods which I regarded as my own, until my own were returned to me. And I spent nineteen days at this port, and each day the Prince of Byblos sent to me, saying, "Depart from my port."

Now while the Prince of Byblos was sacrificing to the gods, one of his chief pages was seized by Amun and he told the Prince, "Bring the God into the Light, Bring the Messenger of Amun who is with him, cause him to depart." And while the man was having a seizure, I found a ship that was bound for Egypt, and I placed all that was mine on board the ship, ready to depart. Then the captain of the port came to me and said, "Wait till tomorrow by order of the Prince of Byblos." And I said to him, "Are you not he who has come to me daily saying 'depart from my port'. And if I wait till this ship leaves, then will you not come to me and say 'depart quickly'." And the captain of the port told this to the Prince and he sent to the captain of the ship saying, "Wait till tomorrow morning by order of the Prince."

And in the morning he sent for me, at the time of the morning sacrifice, and he had me brought to the castle where he lives by the edge of the Great Syrian Sea. And he brought me to an upper chamber, where he sat with his back resting against a balcony, and the waves of the Great Syrian Sea beat behind him, and I said to him, "By the favour of Amun" and he said to me, "How long is it since you left the place where Amun is?" And I replied, "Five months and a day up till today." And he said, "Come speak the truth, where are the orders from Amun that you should have, where is the letter of the high-priest of Amun, that should be in your hand?" And I said, "I gave them to Smendes and Tenet-Amun." And he became angry and he said "Where is that vessel of acacia wood that Smendes gave to you? Where is your ship and crew of Syrians? Did he not give you to this ship's captain, at the time of your departure and order him to throw you into the sea. And if this should be so, who would bother themselves about you?" And I said to him, "Was it not an Egyptian crew, and an Egyptian ship, that sailed with me at the order of Smendes, for there are not with him any Syrian crews." And he replied to me, "Are there not twenty vessels lying in my port in communication with Smendes? And at Sidon, that other town that you wish to visit, are there not ten thousand vessels there which are chartered from Tjeker to go to Smendes." I was silent at this serious moment so that he resumed and said, "What commission have you come here to undertake?" And I said, "I have come to collect the wood to build the august boat of Amun-Re, King of the Gods. And that which your father did and his father before him, was to supply wood for this vessel, and will you do the same?" Thus I spoke to him and he replied, "That which they did, I will do. Formerly my ancestors did this because the King of Egypt caused six ships full of the merchandise of Egypt to be unloaded into their ware-house. If you will do the same for me, I will do the same for you." And he had the records of his ancestors brought and they were read before me, and he found that in all 1000 deben of silver were inscribed on his register in payment. And he said, "Now I am not your servant, and I am not the servant of those that sent you. If I call, the cedars of Lebanon will be stretched by the side of the sea, but only if you show me suitable vessels that you have brought for their transport, with the requisite sails, and cords, that you bring to bind the beams that I will cut you for gifts. But if you do not have suitable ships and sails and cordage to carry the wood, your vessels will sink in the sea, and you yourself will die." But I replied, "There are no vessels that do not belong to Amun; the sea is his, and the cedars of Lebanon are his, though you say that they are yours - but covert not the things that belong to Amun-Re, King of the Gods, for the lion loves his own. Now cause my scribe to be sent to me, that I may send him to Smendes and Tenet-Amun, the protectors whom Amun has placed at the north of his country that he may cause to be brought all that I say 'Let it be brought' before I return to the south, and dispatch your miserable remnants, all in all." Thus I spoke, and I gave my letter to his messenger, and he placed on a ship, the beams for the bows, the stern and four other beams shaped with a hatchet, seven pieces in all, and he sent them to Egypt.

His messenger went to Egypt, and he returned to me in Djahy in the first month of winter. Smendes and Tentet-Amun had sent four jugs and a basin of gold, five jugs of silver, ten pieces of linen for making ten cloaks, five hundred rolls of papyrus, five hundred ox-hides, five hundred cords, twenty sacks of lentils and thirty bales of dried fish. And Tentet-Amun sent me five pieces of royal linen for cloaks, a sack of lentils, and five bales of dried fish. The Prince of Byblos rejoiced, and he levied three hundred men, and three hundred oxen, and he put officers at their head to cut down the trees; and they felled them, and the trees lay on the ground all the winter; then in the third month of the Harvest, they were brought to the sea coast. The Prince came and stood near them and said to me "Come". And I went up to him and he spoke and said, "See the commission that my father executed of old, I too have done. The wood is here even to the last piece, now do according to your heart's desire and load it for Egypt. For see I have not done to you what was done to the envoys of Khamose who dwelt seventeen years in this country and who died here." And I went down to the sea-shore, and I saw eleven vessels that were coming in from the sea, and they were of the Tjeker. And they said to the Prince of Byblos, "Let him be imprisoned; let there be no boat of his that goes down to Egypt."

And I sat down and wept and the secretary of the Prince came to me and he said, "What is the matter?" and I said, "Do you not see those herons that go down to Egypt? Behold! they return to fresh waters; but alas how long shall I be abandoned? For see, these people have come to imprison me again?" Then he went and spoke to the prince, and he was sorry for me, and he sent me two jugs of wine, and he caused Tantanuit, a girl singer of Egypt to be brought to me, to cheer up my heart and sing to me. And he sent a message to me saying, "Eat, drink and be merry, and hear all that I have to say tomorrow morning." And in the morning he sent for his people to come to the landing place, and he stood in the middle of them and he said to the Tjeker, "What is the manner of your coming to this place?" And they said to him, "We have come in pursuit of those broken vessels that you are sending to Egypt with your accursed comrades." And he said to them, "I cannot hold the messenger of Amun captive in my country. I must let him go. Behold! when he is outside my territorial waters you can pursue him." And he loaded my ships and came with me to the harbour of the sea.

After Wen-Amun sailed, he was thrown by a storm upon the island of Alasiya (Cyprus) only some 120 miles from Byblos. And the inhabitants of the land were about to kill him. But Wen-Amun forced his way through the crowd to the house of the Princess of Cyprus and threw himself at her feet. And he said, "Does anyone here speak Egyptian?" And one said that they did. And Wen-Amun said that injustice was done in all places, but that Alasiya had a reputation for justice. So that the princess asked what he meant, and he replied that her people wished to kill his sailors from Byblos when he had been thrown on her island by a storm, and that if this was done Zikar-Baal would kill ten crews of theirs in reply. And the princess told the people to be quiet and she said to Wen-Amun, "Be at rest . . ."

At this point the papyrus breaks off. However, he must have returned safely to Egypt or the papyrus would not have been found there.

27   HELEN IN EGYPT

This story is told in Herodotus *Book II*, chapters 112, 113, 115-120.

After Paris carriéd off Helen from Sparta, he was taken by adverse winds to the Canopic mouth of the Nile. There is on the coast a temple to Heracles (Horus) with a right of asylum. When they heard this, many of the sailors from the ship went and took refuge there, because they feared the wrath of the gods for what Paris had done to Helen, and the injury to Menelaus. They accused Paris of having broken his word to his host and laid a complaint about him before the Warden of the Nile Mouths whose name was Thounis.

When the warden had received this report, he sent at once to the king to inform him of what had taken place, telling him Paris had deceived his host in Greece and run off with his wife, as well as stolen a lot of treasure. Then the king sent word that this could not be allowed, for it was pleasing neither to gods nor men. So the Egyptian officials seized the ships and impounded them and took Paris and Helen and all their crew to Memphis. Paris told him that he was a son of the King of Troy but when asked how he came by Helen, he made an evasive answer. But his crew gave the correct account to the king. The king was very angry and said that if he had not made it a rule never to sacrifice any stranger who came to the coast of Egypt washed up by the sea, he would have executed Paris for what he had done. But there was no need for him to profit by his act, and he would have to depart in three days if he was to avoid being killed.

Meanwhile, Helen was kept in the temple of Aphrodite (Hathor) and her treasure too. Some say the *Ka* (double) of Helen was sent with Paris to Troy, others that he went back empty

100

handed. Anyway many years later when Menelaus was sailing back from Troy after its sack, he too was blown by adverse winds to the coast of Egypt and his boat wrecked, and he and some of his crew cast ashore. Then he too took refuge in the sanctuary of the temple and heard that Helen was dwelling nearby in the temple of Aphrodite. Then he met her and they made a plan together. For the old Egyptian king had died and the young one, who had ascended the throne, wished to marry the most beautiful woman in the world, which Helen then was. She had always refused him as she said she did not know if her husband was still alive. But she arranged with Menelaus that they should tell the king that Menelaus had died

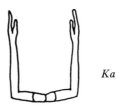

Ka

and that he (Menelaus) had brought to Egypt the news of his own death. Then Helen said that she would marry the king but that first she must carry out the requisite rites for the soul of her dead husband. To do this, she must have wine and offerings and a bull to sacrifice, and a ship to take her and Menelaus and the Greek sailors beyond the Egyptian territorial waters, so that a sacrifice might be made on the neutral sea. So the king agreed, and a ship was made ready for Helen, and she and Menelaus and as many of the Greek crew as were left embarked on the ship. And when they had sailed out of sight of land, they threw overboard the Egyptians who were accompanying them and some of these managed to swim back to land and tell the king that he had lost his prospective bride.

This legend is well known to the modern Greeks and was made use of by George Seferis in his poem *Helen*:

On a night such as this, by the shore of Proteus,
the Spartan slave girls heard you and danced their lament,
and among them - who would have thought it? - Helen!
She whom we hunted so many years by the banks of the
    Scamander.

She was there, at the desert's lip; I touched her; she spoke to me:
'It isn't true, it isn't true', she cried.
'I didn't board the blue-bowed ship.
I never went to valiant Troy.'

Deep-girdled, the sun in her hair, and that stature
shadows and smiles everywhere,
on shoulders, thighs, and knees;
the skin alive, and her eyes
with the large eyelids,
all were there, on the banks of a Delta.

                                        And at Troy?
At Troy, nothing; a phantom image.
The gods wanted it so.
And Paris, Paris lay with a shadow as though it were a solid form.
And we slaughtered ourselves for Helen ten long years.

Great suffering had come to Greece.
So many bodies thrown
to the jaws of the sea, to the jaws of the earth
so many souls
fed to the millstones like grain.
And the rivers swelled, the blood bedded in muck,
all for a linen undulation, a bit of cloud,
a butterfly's flicker, a swan's down,
an empty tunic - all for a Helen . . .

28   THE TREASURE CHAMBER
OF KING RHAMPSINTUS

According to Herodotus *Book II*, chapter 121, there was once a king of Egypt called Rhampsintus who was very rich and who worried in case his treasure should be stolen, so he got his architect to construct a treasure chamber made of stone next to the palace. The clever builder to whom he entrusted the work did so, but contrived to make a secret entry to the treasure chamber by making a stone that would turn at the touch, but which looked just like the rest of the wall. He then fell ill, but before he died he sent for his two sons who were builders like himself and told them what he had done. As soon as he had died the young men got into the chamber and removed some of the king's treasure. But they were not very skilful in disguising what they had done, and the next time that the king visited his treasure he saw that some of the chests were empty.

It was not long before the men had squandered what they had got, and went back for more. The king found this out also, but could not find the way they got in or out. So he set traps inside and next time the brothers climbed in one of them was caught in the trap. His brother could not release him, so the unfortunate youth told his brother to cut off his head and make off, so that the king would not know who had done this thing. This he did and the king was very surprised to find a headless body in the trap and still more treasure missing.

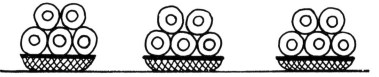

Gold treasure

To find out who did it the king had the man's body hung beside the city wall and put a guard of soldiers upon it to catch anyone who tried to come and take it away. The thief's mother was very upset at this treatment of her son's body, and she told her surviving son that he must make some attempt to obtain his brother's body. So the youth devised a plan. He loaded his donkeys with wine skins and drove them along the road where the body was hanging. When he got near the soldiers he contrived to loosen one of the ties and let the wine run out. He then cried aloud and beat his breast, running from one of the donkeys to the other trying to secure their loads. The guards seeing the wine running into the roadway straightway took vessels and caught some of the wine. At first he abused the guards saying it was their fault that he was losing his wine, but then he made it up with them and gave them another wine skin and they all sat down together to drink it. Soon the guards got very drunk and went to sleep where they were. When night fell the young man cut down his brother's body, put it in a sack that he had brought with him, and took it away.

The king was therefore determined to find out who had done this to him, so he, so the story goes, though Herodotus thinks it very unlikely, made his daughter act as a prostitute and accept every man who came to visit her. The only thing she asked of them was that instead of payment the client should tell her what was the cleverest thing he had done, and what was his greatest crime. The thief on hearing this determined to outwit her as well. He therefore got the hand and arm of a newly dead man; this he placed under his cloak. He then went to visit the princess. When asked what he had done he said his greatest crime was cutting off his brother's head when caught in the king's trap, and his cleverest act was getting hold of his brother's dead body. The princess tried to grab hold of him, but the thief gave her the dead man's hand to hold, and he escaped in the darkness.

The king was astonished when he heard about this and had a proclamation made offering the thief immunity if he would come forward and confess. This the youth did and was richly rewarded. Some say he even married the princess, but this is unlikely as the Egyptian kings did not marry off their daughters to commoners, however clever they may have been.

This inscription was carved in thirty-two columns on the face of a cracked granite boulder situated on the island of Sehal in the First Cataract, south of Aswan. It was found by an American amateur Egyptologist, C. Wilbour, in 1889, and after his death his collection formed the basis of the Brooklyn Museum. The rock was already split when the inscription was cut; it has suffered further damage since. Above the text is a relief of King Zozer making offerings to Khnum-Re, Satet and Anuket. The text is important as it served to connect Zozer with his Horus name, and so enabled the builder of the Step Pyramid to be finally identified. Although purporting to be a text of Third Dynasty date, it is thought to be a Ptolemaic copy, though it may have been based on a genuine Old Kingdom original.

It begins, "Year eighteen of the Horus Neterkhet (Zozer), the King of Upper and Lower Egypt. Zozer was mourning in his palace because the Nile had not risen for seven years and there was a famine in all the land. There was no grain in the royal stores. All kinds

Hapi, God of the Inundation

of food had become scarce, and men had become weak so that they could not go about searching for sustenance. Everyone was in distress. There were no offerings to give to the temples. Young and old alike suffered.

"Zozer enquired of his chief of works, Imhotep, as to where Hapi rose. He was unable to say, but he consulted the priests at 'The Temple of the Net', which was one of the names for the temple of Thoth at Hermopolis. Imhotep's lector priest went quickly to Hermopolis and consulted the sacred books, from which he learnt that the headwaters of the river rose at Elephantine, the First Nome of Upper Egypt, bordering on Lower Nubia (Wawat), to the south.

"The river traditionally was said to rise in two caverns where dwelt Hapi, but Khnum, the ram-headed god of the cataract, controlled its flow as he held the bolt of the door in his hand. He was known as Lord of the Fields because he supplied the water for the crops, controlled the fowl and the fish of the river. He controlled not only the Nubians to the south, but the quarries that lay round the First Cataract. It is here that the stone was obtained for the temples of Egypt and the statues of the gods and the kings.

"Zozer, having learnt that Khnum was the god who controlled the waters of the Nile, made the god an offering, and slept in the temple. There he had a dream wherein Khnum appeared to him in a kindly fashion. The god addressed him saying, 'I am Khnum your maker. My arms are around you to steady you, and to save you. I give you the rock to build your temples, and rebuild those which have fallen into disrepair. I am the Creator God who fashioned mankind on my wheel, but of recent years my shrines have fallen into decay and no offerings have been made to me. If this is remedied, the Nile will rise again.'

"Zozer was delighted to find the cause of the trouble and he hurried to make a decree in favour of Khnum. He offered him control of all the land on both sides of the river as far as Takompso, a region extending twelve stadia (a Greek measure) south of Elephantine. He gave him control of all the fishermen and hunters of the region, possession of all the land and the tenant farmers who were working there, as well as all mineral rights and one-tenth of gold, ivory, ebony, carob wood, carnelian and all precious stones that were found there. As Elephantine was the trading post with Wawat and the south, this gave Khnum a very large revenue. The temple was also to have one-tenth of the dues from the royal quarries, and all that was necessary was to be supplied to the temple." This was a tremendous benefaction and would have made the Khnum priesthood one of the richest in the land.

This is one of several accounts of famines in the Egyptian texts, some of which predate the Biblical account by many centuries.

The legend of the hoopoes comes from Robert Curzon's *Visits to the Monasteries of the Levant* which he undertook in 1833. He found that the Arabs regarded all the animals and birds as being ruled by individual kings. Thus when he visited Egypt, he was told that the king of the crocodiles was supposed to reside in the Nile at Assyout.

Now the hoopoe is a small bird rather like a woodcock but on its head it bears a beautiful crown of golden feathers, which it can move at will, and this story tells how the hoopoes got their crowns.

King Solomon used to travel over his dominions by means of a magic carpet, square in shape with a long fringe and supported by four djinni of the air; and to sit on, he had a magnificent, ivory throne, but unfortunately it had no canopy. One very hot day, he suffered greatly from the rays of the sun, which burnt his arms and neck. Now King Solomon, by virtue of his seal, had control over djinni, animals and birds so that when he saw a flock of vultures flying past, he called to them to fly above his head and shield him from the sun. The vultures were not willing to do this as they were flying northwards and Solomon was going in the other direction. So they refused. Solomon was furious and he cursed the birds. "O impious birds, because you will not obey the command of your lord who rules over the whole world, the feathers of your necks shall fall off; and the heat of the sun, and the coldness of winter, and the keenness of the wind and the beating of the rain shall fall upon your rebellious necks, which shall not be protected with feathers like the necks of other birds. Whereas you have up until now lived well, henceforth you shall eat carrion and feed upon offal. Your race shall be impure until the end of the world."

Fortunately for Solomon, a flock of hoopoes were also flying past at that time, so the King called to them asking them to come and fly between him and the sun to shelter him from its rays. The king of the hoopoes replied that his birds were rather small, but that he would collect as many as possible and try and form a canopy for the King. This they did, and formed a very effective one. When the journey was over and King Solomon had returned to his palace, he sent for the king of the hoopoes and asked what reward they would like. But the king of the hoopoes was confused by the bustle of the court and the honour of standing before Solomon, so he asked for time to consider the matter. His request was granted. He then returned to consult his wife and family about a suitable reward. He also enquired from the council of the chief

Hoopoe

hoopoes about this matter. However, it was very difficult for them to decide what they would like. Some wished to be larger and some wished to be more brightly coloured, but there was no unanimity. So the queen called the king aside and suggested that as they had protected King Solomon's head from the sun, gold crowns on their heads would be a suitable reward. This, she felt, would set them apart from all the other birds. The king of the hoopoes who had secretly admired King Solomon's crown while flying overhead, thought this was a good idea and put the suggestion to Solomon.

However, Solomon did not think that this was a good idea, as in his wisdom he foresaw what would happen, and told the hoopoe

109

that he was a foolish bird to ask for such a thing. But the hoopoe was adamant in his request, so Solomon could only suggest that if things went wrong, he was to return to him for help.

So all the hoopoes had gold crowns, of which they were exceedingly proud. They went down to the rivers and lakes and greatly admired their reflection in the waters. The queen of the hoopoes took to sitting on a branch of a tree and refused to speak to the bee-eaters who were cousins of theirs and other birds who had previously been her friends. One of the fowlers noticed this odd behaviour, and placed a broken mirror in his trap to catch one. When he had caught one, he saw the golden crown and took the bird to a metalsmith to ask what metal it was. The metalsmith replied brass, and only offered a little money for the bird, but asked the fowler to bring him any others that he caught, which he duly did. One day he met another merchant and showed him several crowns, and then discovered that they were really made of gold. It led to people going out to catch the hoopoes by every kind of method, bird-lime, traps and arrows. This nearly exterminated the hoopoes and the king of the hoopoes had great trouble reaching the palace of King Solomon for help and had to fly by night, to avoid being caught.

With floods of tears and many groans he told of the awful fate that had befallen his people through their vanity. King Solomon was sorry for him, and offered to exchange the gold crowns for ones made of golden feathers, which offer the king of the hoopoes gratefully accepted. From this time onwards, the hoopoes have increased and flourished, and instead of being afraid of men have tended to nest near human habitation.

31   *QUEEN BALKIS AND THE HOOPOES*

This is another story told about King Solomon, it is based on one from the Koran.

As everyone knows, King Solomon, on whose name be peace, understood the language of the birds, beasts and fishes, and controlled them as he did the djinn. When he wished to travel on his silken carpet that had been woven specially for him by a djinn, a strong wind raised it into the air, then a gentle breeze carried it along. One day King Solomon was seated on his throne, with his head shaded by various birds whom he summoned to protect him from the rays of the sun, as told in the previous story.

Solomon could hear everything that anyone said as he passed over head. One day he passed over the Valley of the Ants, which was in a desert area. The king of the ants was alarmed when he saw the large carpet flying through the air and called out to his subjects "Go into your houses lest those wretches who are flying overhead descend and tread upon you." So King Solomon delayed his descent until all the ants had taken cover, then he brought the carpet down to have some rest and refreshment, as he was very hot and thirsty and wanted some water after passing over so much desert. He called for the hoopoe bird, which has to have a lot of water and always knows where it is to be found, because if it does not have plenty of moisture its beak splits and it cannot pick up its food and dies of starvation. But the hoopoe could not be found anywhere.

The king of the hoopoes, who was accompanying King Solomon, saw that he was greatly interested in the areas over which he was passing and thought he would go away and find some further information about them. He flew into the air and went a long way south until he saw some beautiful gardens. These belonged to Queen Balkis who was the ruler of the Yemen. He thought he would like to find out more about her, and on landing met another hoopoe who lived in her garden, who said that he would show him round. At first the king of the hoopoes thought that he had better not stay in case King Solomon should miss him, but the other bird persuaded him and they spent a delightful day in the shade of the trees while he learned all about the Yemen.

Meanwhile, King Solomon, who was very cross to find the hoopoe missing, ordered the eagle, the king of the birds, to go and look for him. The eagle soared into the sky and saw far, far away to the south-west the king of the hoopoes returning. When he got nearer, the eagle tried to sieze the hoopoe, but he evaded him. The eagle then said to the hoopoe, "I hope that you have a good excuse for your absence or the King will surely kill you."

Verreaux's eagle

The hoopoe then flew down with the eagle and settled in front of King Solomon's throne. He carefully dropped his tail and wings to salute the King. Solomon said he would punish the bird for his absence, but the hoopoe replied, "O King, at the day of judgement you will stand before the throne of Allah, as I stand before you today. Therefore, show me the sort of mercy that you would wish to receive on that day." So King Solomon, thinking of his own fate listened to what the hoopoe had to say.

Then the king of the hoopoes told King Solomon all that he had seen and heard about in the Kingdom of the Yemen, and how beautiful Queen Balkis was. He told Solomon about her bed of gold and silver inlaid with jewels, and that she and her people were unbelievers, who worshipped the sun and the moon, and in particular the moon god, Wad. All this raised the curiosity of King Solomon and he determined to enter into communication with Queen Balkis. He therefore sent the king of the hoopoes with a letter to her.

With the help of his friend, the hoopoe in the Queen's garden, the king of the hoopoes learnt that Queen Balkis always put the keys of the seven doors, that lay between her and the outside door, under her pillow when she went to bed. Her bedroom window faced east so that she was awakened each morning by the rays of the rising sun. So the resident hoopoe advised Solomon's hoopoe that the best way to get the letter to her personally was to stand at the window and block out the light to delay her awakening. In that way he could see for himself how beautiful she was and give her the letter. The bird did this, and the Queen was astonished to see a strange hoopoe at her window, but took the letter and read it. Then she called her councillors together and told them about it and how Solomon said that he wished to establish friendly relations with Queen Balkis, but that she and her people must give up the worship of the sun and the moon and turn to the one true god.

Queen Balkis decided first to test the wisdom of Solomon of which she had heard so much. So she sent him some gifts that would present problems. She sent to him three hundred boys and girls, slaves, all dressed alike, and asked him to pick out which were the boys and which were the girls. She also sent some pierced and unpierced precious stones in a casket and asked him to thread them all without the help of men or of djinn. Finally she sent him four bricks of solid gold to show him how rich she was.

The hoopoe flew back to King Solomon and told him all that had occurred. Solomon ordered the djinn to build a road paved with gold blocks but to leave four places empty. This they did, and it was ready by the time Queen Balkis's messenger arrived. He was rather amazed to find a whole road of gold bricks and sadly fitted Queen Balkis's four bricks into the empty space. When he presented the gifts, Solomon knew at once what was in the casket, and called a worm and ordered it to pierce each of the unpierced jewels. This the worm did and Solomon asked what it wanted most, and the worm replied, "To live in trees", and there the tree-worm lives to this day. Then Solomon called up a white maggot and ordered him to thread the precious stones, which he did. Solomon asked him the same question, what did he want most, and the maggot replied, "To live always in fruit", and the white maggot lives in fruit to this day.

Then King Solomon ordered the boy and girl slaves to be brought before him, and basins of water placed before them so that they might wash. The girls took the water first in one hand and then in the other and rubbed it on their faces, but the boys took the water in both hands and splashed it on their faces. The girls washed their arms from the elbows down to the wrists, but the boys from the wrists to the elbows. Thus did Solomon easily distinguish the boys from the girls.

Then King Solomon ordered the messenger to take all the presents back to Queen Balkis and tell her that if she and her people were not converted to the worship of Allah he would destroy them. However, when King Solomon finally saw Queen Balkis, he fell in love with her and married her, and she kept all the gold she had given him and more. Peace be on them.

One day when the late Director General of Antiquities, Gaston Maspero, was working at the Ramesseum, he overheard the following story told by one of the guards.

There was once a Sultan of Luxor who lived in the Temple of Luxor, then known as the palace or castle. Not far from this place there was a poor man who made what money he could by trading linen. He lived in a single room, and had only dry bread to eat, except when his only fig tree, which grew in his courtyard, put forth some figs. One day when he returned home, he saw that his tree had suddenly produced the most splendid figs. There were ten of these and the first was already ripe. These figs were so much better than any the tree had produced before that he went immediately to his neighbour the *rammal*, the sand diviner who told fortunes in sand, who took his box of sand, made some lines in the sand and announced to the man that "Every day for ten days you must take one of your figs to the Sultan. On the tenth day your destiny will be fulfilled, and the good and the wicked will both find their proper place."

The Sultan of Luxor, like all the best Sultans, used to hold an audience every day. He began at sunrise and used to sit outside the first court between the two obelisks (this was before the French had taken away one of the obelisks to stand in Paris). Here he used to sit and listen to petitions, grievances and the difficulties of his subjects, aided by his vizier. Sometimes he did not hesitate to beat his more recalcitrant subjects. This audience went on every day till twelve o'clock when, convinced that he had done a good day's work, and anxious to have his midday meal, he broke off the sitting and returned to his palace.

The merchant, who had placed his fig on a china plate covered with a napkin, waited patiently from dawn till it was time to come before the Sultan. Then he prostrated himself and offered the fig to the Sultan, saying that God had favoured him by sending him ten magnificent figs out of season, and that as a result he felt that he had to offer them to the Sultan, as they were obviously intended for no ordinary mortal to eat. He therefore proposed to bring one every morning to the Sultan as they ripened. The Sultan, who highly approved of these sentiments, ate the fig, found it excellent and ordered the vizier, who stood behind him, to arrange for the man to be given a present in the form of a *galibiah* and some money. The poor man immediately went home, he laid in the means of a splendid feast with pigeons, lamb, iced drinks, and bought himself a white donkey. He then asked in all the neighbours and told them of his good luck.

Branch of fig tree

Next day the poor man took the next fig to the Sultan, and every succeeding day until only three figs were left. Every day the Sultan piled more and more gifts upon him, slaves, camels, land, gold and silver until the vizier got jealous and thought that the treasury was being unnecessarily depleted. He therefore cast about in his mind for a way to put an end to the situation. He went to the poor man's house by night and said to him, "The Sultan talks of you unceasingly, he even thinks of giving you his daughter in marriage, but one thing holds him back. You obviously eat a great deal of garlic and he dislikes the smell very much. It would be a good idea if you tied up your face in a shawl next time you come with your fig." So the next morning the poor man arrived with his head all muffled up. When he was going away, the Sultan asked the vizier what this meant. "I do not know", said the vizier, "but if it please Your Majesty I will find out." He hurried away, but not to ask the poor man as he already knew the answer. Finally he returned to the Sultan with a very long face, and refused for some time to reply to his questions. Finally, he replied, prostrating himself before the ruler. "I hardly like to tell your Majesty, but remember we are dealing with a poor uneducated man whose manners are not as good as one might hope for. He says he is very grateful to your Majesty for the gifts, but that he cannot stand the smell of your Majesty's breath, and he only avoids fainting by covering up his head." The Sultan was furious at this suggestion, but he suddenly burst out laughing and said, "It does not matter, I do not want to be in his debt, and if he comes again to honour me with his figs, I will give him a gift, by the side of which all that he received before will be nothing."

The vizier went home in a very disturbed state fearing that his plan had miscarried, and that he had increased, rather than diminished the favour in which the Sultan held the man. Next day the man appeared as before with his head swathed up. The Sultan looked at him for a little while and then wrote a note and sealed it with his own seal ring. He gave it to the man telling him to go early to the treasury and ask for the chief treasurer, and that he would not regret having done so.

When the audience finished, the vizier who had heard all that had passed joined the man and congratulated him. He then said, "His Majesty is so pleased with you that he wishes to save you the slightest trouble. The note is a command to give you a thousand pounds, but if you give it to me I will give you a thousand pounds to save you the trouble of collecting it; just give me the note in return." The poor man immediately gave up the note in return for the money, and the vizier who thought that he had made his fortune repaired to the treasury as soon as it opened in the morning. The treasurer read the note, kissed the seal and raised his hands and two of the soldiers, who were on guard, immediately cut off the vizier's head before he knew what was happening.

Later when the audience began the Sultan was astonished to see the merchant again in his place, with his head bound up as usual. He looked round to point this out to the vizier, but he was nowhere to be seen. At this point the treasurer entered carrying a leather bag. On seeing him the Sultan said, "Why did you not behead the man I sent you?" The treasurer replied, "Pardon me your Majesty, but I put him to death as you requested, and here is his head." At this he placed the vizier's head in front of the Sultan. "What have you done!" cried the Sultan, "You have killed my minister." "Sire" said the treasurer, "Did you not command me to kill the person who brought me the note?" The Sultan replied "Doubtless, but it was not the vizier who was to bring the note." The treasurer replied, "All the same it was he who brought it." This was not much help to the Sultan, who did not understand what had happened. So they sent for the merchant and asked him to explain, so he did; he told them how the vizier had asked him to tie up his head, and why and how the vizier had given him a thousand pounds in return for the note. The Sultan finally enlightened said, "This vizier was a wicked man, but all's well that ends well. He stole your place, and paid for it with his own life; take his place in your turn and become my vizier."

The merchant bowed to the ground before the Sultan and said, "The *rammal* was right, blessed be the *rammal*!" The Sultan was even more confused and said, "What has the *rammal* to do with this affair?" The merchant replied, "O Sire, when I consulted him, did he not say that on the tenth day the good and the wicked would each end in his proper place? Today is the tenth day, the vizier is dead and I am in the vizier's place!"

118

33   THE LANDING OF NOAH'S ARK

This legend is taken from the story told to R.G. Gayer-Anderson Pasha by Sheikh Sulaiman al-Kretli, and included in his book, *Legends of the Beit al-Kretliya* (House of the Cretan in Cairo).

"In the name of God the compassionate and the merciful." This legend concerns the sacred ground on which both the Beit al-Kretliya and the Ibn al-Talun Mosque were built. This is the Gebel Yashkur, the Hill of Thanksgiving, and the story tells how in early times it and its neighbourhood became blessed and sanctified. It is important to know that the blessed hill on which the house and mosque were built was at one time very much higher than it is now. It was in fact the highest point in Egypt rising to a considerable height, and it was on the peak of this mountain and not on Mount Ararat, as some have supposed, that the Blessed Ark came to rest after the flood had subsided.

"You will of course recall when Father Noah, after the revelation of Allah about the destruction of the world, was building his ark, all those that passed by jeered at him and taunted him saying, 'For what purpose are you making such a large ship.' To this Noah made no reply but went on steadily with his boat-building. Soon afterwards the waters rose, all mankind was turned to clay and that vile generation was drowned in the Deluge.

"Noah, as I have said, together with his wife, his sons and their wives were saved and stepped from the Ark onto Gebel Yashkur, together with every kind of beast, male and female, to replenish the earth. For had not God said to Noah, 'O Noah! Disembark with peace from Us and with blessings on you and all peoples to be born from those who are with You.' So they set up the first city of Cairo (known as Misr to the Egyptians). That was the first

119

city to be built after the flood, although there had been many cities before then built by the ancient Kings of Egypt, who had also hewn a deep well through the rock of Gebel Yashkur. It was into this well called the Bir al-Watawit, the "Well of the Bats", now in the courtyard of the Beit al-Kretliya, that the last of the Deluge subsided, for had not God said, "O Earth swallow up thy waters. O Heaven cease!" Ever since that time it has been regarded as a Holy Well.

The "Well of Bats"

"Let me tell you there is no doubt whatever that it was here that these marvellous events took place. (The Koran says of this event 'And the water abated, and the decree was fulfilled and the Ark rested upon Mount Judi.' We do not know exactly where Mount Judi is, but it is said to be Gebel Yashkur).

"Now when the great Ibn Talun came to build his mosque, Noah's Ark was still stranded high and dry here on Gebel Yashkur, a record of Noah's landing and undoubted proof that the Ark rested here after the Flood in days long since gone by, for such was God's will."

120

34   THE BENEVOLENT SERPENT

This is another legend connected with the Beit al-Kretliya next to the Ibn Talun Mosque.

Every ancient house in Cairo has many stories associated with it, and this tale is about a friendly serpent. Serpents dwell only in houses that are especially favoured by God. Such snakes are guardians and keep the house in their care allowing no other reptile to enter or any evil to be harboured there. Normally the "guardian" is never seen, as it ventures forth only at night or in secret when everyone is out. However, the young of the serpent are not so careful and sometimes ill may befall them.

This is the adventure that befell the young of the "guardian" of the Beit al-Kretliya. Once, a long time ago when the Hajj Mahummad was living in the house, his two little children playing in the courtyard saw the two small snakes, who had ventured out of their hiding place. The boys pounced on them and tied them up with string and played with them, unaware of the danger that they were in. Not long afterwards, the mother snake returned and being unable to find her children, searched for them everywhere. She soon found them in the courtyard captives of the two small boys. She became very angry and as she could not easily rescue them, decided on taking revenge. So she went to the *zir* which is a water-jar with a pointed base that stands in the courtyard of every Egyptian house, and into it spat her venom, so that anyone drinking from the *zir* would die of poison.

Hardly had she done so when Hajj Mahummad returned home. He was horrified to see his sons playing with the little snakes and immediately rebuked them saying, "O wicked ones! Shame on you! Do you not know that you have made captive the little ones of our patron and protectress, our benevolent serpent without whose blessing this house would surely be destroyed. In the name of the Prophet, release your victims at once lest greater harm befall you and all of us." The boys were very much afraid at this rebuke and hastened to release the young snakes, who wriggled away into the crack in which they lived.

Snake and Zir

The benevolent serpent, who had been lurking nearby, heard all that had been said and she was delighted to welcome back the small snakes who were unharmed, although very much affrighted. She realised that neither the Hajj nor his sons wished her or her offspring any harm and she felt ashamed that she had poisoned the house's drinking water. She wondered what she could do to prevent something untoward taking place. She was even more alarmed when she heard the Hajj calling to the servant girl, Aisha, to fetch him a cup of cold water from the *zir*. To prevent harm coming to him, the serpent hastened to the cupboard where the *zir* was kept, and wrapping herself round the jar she squeezed and squeezed until it broke and the water gushed out, and the inhabitants of the house were saved from being poisoned. The people of the house were greatly amazed at the jar breaking, as it had broken into ninety-nine pieces, a magical number. They thought it had been the work of a djinn or an *afrit*. They never realised that their lives had been saved by the act of the benevolent serpent.

This tale comes from the *Arabian Nights* and is set in Alexandria and abroad and embodies the story told between the nights nine hundred and thirty and nine hundred and forty, about how Abu-Kir Bay got its name.

There were in the city of Alexandria two men, one of whom was a dyer called Abu-Kir, the other a barber called Abu-Sir. They were neighbours and had adjoining shops. Abu-Sir was an honest man, whereas the dyer was a swindler, a liar and a person of extreme wickedness. It was his custom when anyone asked him to dye a piece of stuff to ask for the price in advance, and say that he was going to buy materials to do the dyeing with the money so obtained. However, instead of doing this, he went out and bought the best of everything to eat and drink. When the customer returned to ask for his material back, he would make some excuse saying, come back tomorrow, I had guests today, or my daughter was getting married, or my wife gave birth to a child. He thus put off his creditors from day to day. When he could no longer do so, he said that he had dyed the material and obtained an excellent result, but that while it was drying someone had stolen it. As a result nothing could be obtained from him, even when threatened by the Kadi (judge). He therefore became notorious in this quarter and had such a bad reputation that no one would employ him. As a result he took to sitting all day in the shop of his friend Abu-Sir, the barber. There were, however, a few people who did not know of his reputation and who still asked for his services, which enabled him to gain an uncertain living. One day he stole the cloth of a violent man, who threatened his life.

Meanwhile, his neighbour Abu-Sir, who was also very poor, was desirous of travelling as he thought conditions for him might be better elsewhere. He finally persuaded Abu-Kir to accompany him. They made an agreement that they were to be as brothers and that whoever found employment would support the other. They embarked that day on a ship bound for a distant port. By good chance there was not another barber on board, and the passengers numbered one hundred and twenty, without counting the captain and crew. The barber then said to the dyer, "We are now at sea, we have only brought a few provisions with us, so I will therefore go about among the passengers and see if I can get any custom, and in lieu of payment I will ask them to give us food and drink so we shall not starve on the way." He then went out among the passengers with the tools of his trade and it was not long before he was being asked to shave some of them. When they offered him payment he refused, and asked for food and drink. The bread and cheese so obtained, he took back to where Abu-Kir was resting. Abu-Kir was sleeping most of the time but woke up to eat with enjoyment all that Abu-Sir brought. Before sunset Abu-Sir had collected thirty loaves of bread as well as cheese, olives and batarikh (a dish made of the roe of salt fish).

Abu-Sir then shaved the captain and took the opportunity of telling him how they had embarked without proper provisions for the voyage. The captain who was a good man asked Abu-Sir to eat at his table every night and to bring his companion, but Abu-Kir feigned sea-sickness. Although he consumed the provisions that Abu-Sir had obtained from the passengers, he refused to go and eat with the captain. Abu-Sir did go to dinner and found the captain sitting at a table with over twenty dishes before him. The captain, when he had enquired after Abu-Kir, put aside a kebab dish and put into it some of every kind of food for Abu-Sir to take to his friend after dinner. Although it was enough for ten men Abu-Kir demolished it all as though he had been a ravenous lion. This continued for twenty days, and always Abu-Sir brought to Abu-Kir a full plate from the captain's table and always Abu-Kir ate it avidly and went back to sleep, and did nothing for the whole voyage.

When the ship moored in the harbour of a city, they both got off and went to a khan and took a room there. Abu-Sir furnished it with all that they needed and went out and bought the necessary provisions. He then cooked these and all the time Abu-Kir slept. He only woke up when Abu-Sir remonstrated with him, but he said he felt giddy and could not move. On the forty-first day the barber fell sick and could not go out to earn money, so he engaged the doorkeeper of the khan to get them some food, but soon he became so ill that he could no longer attend to this and became delirious.

Consequently, Abu-Kir became very hungry, so he searched the clothing of Abu-Sir and found some money which he took and went out closing the door behind him. He went to the suq and bought himself a costly outfit, but he found all the clothes were blue and white. So he took a handkerchief to a dyer and asked him to dye it. The dyer said it would cost twenty pieces of silver; Abu-Kir said that it would be done in his country for two pieces of silver. Then he asked what colour the man would dye it, and the reply was blue, but Abu-Kir said he wanted red, but the dyer said he did not know how to dye it red, and it was the same reply everywhere, when he asked for other colours, like green or yellow. Abu-Kir then enumerated all the colours to the dyer, who replied, "We in this city are forty masters, not one more not one less, and when one dies we take his son and teach him to be a master, but we only know how to dye the colour blue." Abu-Kir said, "I too

Medieval boat

am a dyer and I know how to dye all colours. I would ask you to take me into your service for pay and I will teach you to dye all the colours." The dyer replied, "We never take strangers into our company ever." Abu-Kir asked what if he opened his own dying shop, but the other said he could not do that either. Then Abu-Kir went round all the forty masters and they all said the same thing. The Sheikh of the Dyers also said, "We do not allow strangers to enter into our trade."

Upon hearing this, Abu-Kir became extremely angry and went to complain to the King of the city. He explained that he was a dyer and could dye red of various types, such as rose colour and jujube colour, green of various hues, like plant green and pistachio green, oil green and parrot's wing green, black such as kohl black and coal black, yellow such as lemon and orange, and proceeded to mention to the King all the various shades. Then he said to the King, "The dyers in your town are unable to dye any of these colours, or anything but blue, but they will not admit me among them as a master or even as a hired hand." The King said, "If you have spoken the truth I will open for you a dyeing shop, and give you support, and as for the other dyers, do not worry about them for I will hang anyone who opposes you, over the door of his shop." He called his master builder and told him to go with Abu-Kir and convert any place he chose into a dyeing shop. He also gave him a splendid robe and a thousand gold pieces to support himself with until the shop was ready. He supplied him with a house and two mamlukes to guard him, and a horse with splendid trappings fit for an emir.

The next day Abu-Kir went forth with the builder and found a place that suited him. The owner was ejected and recompensed by the King, and Abu-Kir had his dyeing shop constructed on the spot. He then asked the King for capital to set up the materials of his trade, and the King gave him four thousand gold pieces. He went out and bought all that was needed and the King sent him five hundred pieces of stuff which he dyed all different colours and spread them out on ropes before the shop door. The people were astounded, never having seen the like and crowds collected, asking him the names of the colours. The King was delighted, as were all the soldiers and he did a roaring trade. He made a lot of money but refused to employ any local dyers, using only black negro slaves. Abu-Kir thus became a rich man.

However, let us return to Abu-Sir. After Abu-Kir had left him, he remained delirious for three days, not knowing where he was. The doorkeeper seeing the closed door and hearing Abu-Sir groaning, opened the door and found him. He showed him the empty purse so that Abu-Sir knew that Abu-Kir had robbed him of all that he had. The doorkeeper was a good man and he supported Abu-Sir through a long illness. At the end of two months the fever broke and he recovered. When he was able to get up he said to the doorkeeper, "If God will enable me I will recompense you", but the doorkeeper replied that he did it for God's sake and wished for no reward. The barber then went out of the khan and chance led him to that part of the suq where Abu-Kir had established his shop. Abu-Sir saw the brightly dyed material and the crowds waiting outside and enquired what was going on. He was told that the King had established a stranger called Abu-Kir there and that it was known as the Sultan's dyeing shop. He was told all that had happened and of the dispute between Abu-Kir and the dyers. Abu-Sir was delighted with his friend's success and thought that he would be warmly greeted. However, Abu-Kir turned on him, smote him with many blows and threatened his life, so that he was forced to go back to the khan to recover.

After he had recovered somewhat, he thought that he would go to the baths to relax, but on enquiring the way to the nearest bath, discovered that the city had none and that the people just washed in the sea. He straightaway craved an audience with the King and told him he was a bathkeeper and described the joys of the bath to the King. The King was amazed and gave him fresh garments and a horse, furnished him with a house and four black slaves and treated him with even more honour than the dyer. Abu-Sir then had a bath built, and acquainted the King when it was finished, and the King provided him with the means of furnishing it. The people had never seen the like before and crowded in to look. Abu-Sir had a fountain made in the court, and had the water in the bath heated. He was given ten young mamlukes to act as bath assistants and instructed them how to rub the people down. After several days he invited the King to the bath and bathed him. The

King had never experienced anything like it before and was delighted. It was arranged that everyone should pay according to his means for the bath and Abu-Sir accumulated much wealth. He arranged for men to come in the morning and women in the afternoon, so that the Queen and her attendants could also come to bathe.

Eventually Abu-Kir heard of the bath and went to it. On recognising Abu-Sir, he pretended that he had been looking for him everywhere and said that he had not recognised him when he had beaten him up earlier. However, privately Abu-Kir decided to destroy Abu-Sir. He went to the King and expressed great relief that he had 'escaped' the dangers of the bath when he had visited it and warned that if the King went there again he would be poisoned. He said that the bathkeeper would come to him with a depilatory powder which was really poisonous and that he was doing this on behalf of the King of the Christians who had promised him a great reward, as well as the release of his wife and children who were in captivity. Now the King believed this story and to put it to the test he went to the bath and Abu-Sir not knowing of his danger, waited upon him and suggested a depilatory. The King was enraged and caused his guards to seize him. He had Abu-Sir's hands bound behind him and had him brought before him. He then sent for the sea-captain who had brought Abu-Sir to the country and said to him, "Take this villain, put him in a sack with two hundred-weight of unslacked lime, take your boat, row to beneath my palace window and when I give the word fling him into the sea." The captain who had become fond of Abu-Sir took him to an island opposite the King's palace and asked him to explain why the King wanted him killed, to which Abu-Sir replied that he had done nothing and could not think of any crime he had committed. The sea captain believed him and told him to remain on the island and that he would try to save him. He was to wait until a *sambuq* was sailing for Alexandria, and that meanwhile he was to cast his net for some fish. These fish were intended for the royal table and it was the duty of the sea captain to oversee their catch daily. This Abu-Sir did and caught a lot. As he was hungry he killed one and on cutting it up he found a seal ring inside it. This, though he did not know it, belonged to the King.

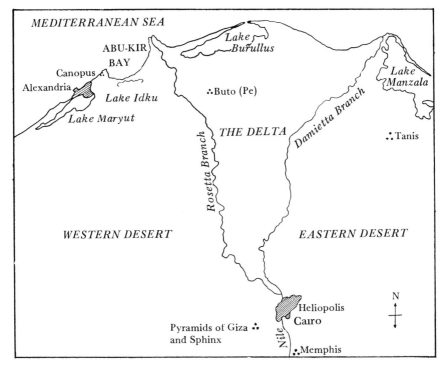

Sketch map of Egypt (Delta area)

The sea captain had substituted a large stone for Abu-Sir, and at a gesture from the King had thrown the sack into the sea as instructed. As the King waved his hand the ring on his finger, to which he owed all his power, slipped into the sea and was swallowed by the fish that Abu-Sir then caught. Abu-Sir put on the King's ring, whose power he did not know, and when two young men came from the royal kitchens to get the fish and asked for the sea captain, Abu-Sir made a gesture with his right hand and the two young men's heads flew off. Abu-Sir was astonished. The captain who returned at that moment, saw the pile of fish, the two dead men and the ring on Abu-Sir's finger. He knew the power of the ring and quickly said to Abu-Sir "O my brother do not move your right hand, for if you do you will kill me." He then took Abu-Sir back to the city for he had nothing further to fear from the King, as he now possessed the King's talisman.

129

Abu-Sir went immediately to the palace where he found the King in a great state of alarm about the loss of his ring. After telling the King the whole story and saying he did not know why the King wished to kill him, he handed back the ring to the King, who was overjoyed. The King then told Abu-Sir the story that the dyer Abu-Kir had told him. Then the King collected together all the witnesses to Abu-Sir's story, such as the doorkeeper of the khan, the sea captain, and the dyers who had seen Abu-Sir being beaten, and sent for Abu-Kir and had him brought before him with his hands bound behind him. The King sentenced him to be thrown into the sea in a sack. Abu-Sir tried to intercede for Abu-Kir, but the King was not prepared to forgive the injuries that he had done to him, so that the execution was carried out.

Abu-Sir asked to be allowed to return to Egypt, and loaded with presents from the King embarked for Alexandria on the sea captain's *sambuq* "The Triumph of Righteousness". After his return one of his mamluks saw a sack lying on the shore nearby and when he opened it found it contained the body of Abu-Kir. Abu-Sir built a tomb for him and the place is known until this day as Abu-Kir Bay.

In Napoleonic times, Abu-Kir Bay saw two great battles, the Battle of the Nile in 1798 when Nelson defeated the French fleet, and in 1799 the land battle, when in Napoleon's presence the French defeated the Turks.

Breasted, James Henry, *Ancient Records of Egypt*, University of Chicago Press, 1906.

Budge, E.A. Wallis, *From Fetish to God in Ancient Egypt*, O.U.P., 1934.

Curzon, Robert, *Visits to Monastries of the Levant*, John Murray, 1881.

Erman, Adolf, *The Literature of the Ancient Egyptians*, Methuen, 1927.

Gayer-Anderson, R.G. "John", *Legends of the Beit al-Kretliya*, East Anglian Daily Times, Ipswich, 1951.

James, T.G.H., *An Introduction to Ancient Egypt*, British Museum, 1979.

Lefebvre, G., *Roman et Contes Egyptiens de l'Epoque Pharaohique*, Paris, 1949.

Lichteim, Miriam, *Ancient Egyptian Literature*, University of California Press, 1974-1978.

Maspero, G., *Egypt : Ancient Sites and Modern Scenes*, T. Fisher Unwin, 1910.

Maspero, G., *Popular Stories of Ancient Egypt*, G.P. Putnam and Sons, 1915.

Petrie, W.M.F., *Egyptian Tales*, Methuen, 1915.

Pritchard, J.B., *Ancient Near Eastern Texts*, Princeton, 1950.

Sale, George, *The Koran* (trans.), Fredrick Warne and Co. N.D.

Sauneron, Serge, *Les Fêtes Religieuses d'Esna,* IFAO, Cairo, 1962.

Anat	Ćanaanite goddess.
Apis Bull	Bull god, manifestation of Ptah of Memphis.
Astarte	Caanite goddess, worshipped at Ras Shamra, identified with Aphrodite.
Atum	Sun god and creator of the universe, shown as an aged man.
Ba-Neb-Tetet	Ram god of Memphis.
Bekhten	A state in North Syria.
Bes	A dwarf god, protector of children.
Busiris	Town in the Delta where Osiris first appeared.
Byblos	City on the coast of Lebanon near the mouth of the Nahr el-Kelb.
Djahy	Lebanon.
Djinn	Airy or fiery bodies, intelligent, imperceptible, capable of appearing in different forms and carrying out heavy labour. They were created of smokeless flame, whereas mankind and the angels, the other two classes of intelligent beings were created of clay and light. They can be saved, and Muhammed the Prophet of God was sent to them as well as to mankind. Their relation to Iblis, the Devil, and other shatains (devils) in general is obscure.
Duat	The Afterworld, usually regarded as being in the west.
Emir	Prince.
Ennead	Group of gods.
Epagnol days	These are the five days at the end of the old Egyptian year on which five of the gods were born.
Geb	The Earth God (human form).
Gebel	Mountain.
Hathor	Cow goddess.
Heket	Frog goddess of birth.
Horus the Behedite	Behedet, place in the northern Delta. Term also used for Horus at Edfu. Shown as a winged sun disc.

132

Horus the Elder	The earliest form of Horus, shown as a hawk-headed man.
Horus the Younger, or Child	Shown as a small boy with the sidelock of youth and with a finger in his mouth.
Ibn-Talun	Ahmed Ibn-Talun was of Turki (Turkish tribe from beyond the Oxus), who was appointed Governor of Egypt in 868 A.D.
Isis	Wife of Osiris and Goddess of Magic (human form).
Justified	Dead.
Ka	A form of the Egyptian soul.
Kadi	Judge or magistrate.
Khan	Inn.
Khepre	Sun god creator in the form of a scarab beetle.
Kharkady	Plant from which a red dye is made and also a drink.
Khnum	The ram-headed god who created man on his potter's wheel, also the god of the First Cataract.
Khonsu	Moon god, third deity of the Triad of Thebes (human form).
King's Jubilee	Traditionally held on the thirtieth year of his reign, and thereafter more frequently.
Lector	Reciting priest.
Mamluke	Slave trained in martial arts.
Meskhenet	Goddess who presided at childbirth.
Metternich Stele	A round topped stone stele presented to Prince Metternich by Mohammed Ali in 1828. Belongs to the type of monument called 'Cippi of Horus' and inscribed with magical spells.
Neith	Creator goddess of Sais, appears in human and bovine form.
Nomes	Greek word for the administrative districts of Ancient Egypt, perpetuated in the modern governorates.
Nun	God personifying the primeval waters.
Nut	Sky goddess (human form, can be shown as a cow).
Obelisk	Stone shaft capped by a pyramidion, usually standing in pairs in front of New Kingdom temples.
Ogdoad	The eight gods of Hermopolis, representing chaos.
Osiris	God of the Underworld.
Pe	One of the twin cities that were the Predynastic capital of Egypt. Modern Tell el-Fara'in.
Persea Tree	The sacred Shoab tree, known as Persea in the Ptolemaic period. Modern Lebbakh.
Ptah	Creator God of Memphis (human form).
Re	The Egyptian Sun God, usually shown as a ram-headed man.
Re-Harakhte	Horus of the horizon.
Retinu	Syria.

Sacred Book of Thoth	Book in which Thoth was reputed to have written down all the wisdom in the world.
Sambuq	Arabian sailing ship.
Sekhmet	Lioness goddess of Memphis, wife of Ptah, guardian of the King.
Seth	God of Chaos.
Shu	God of the Air. Shown with raised arms.
Souls of Pe	The souls of the dead kings.
Suq	Market.
Tanis	City in the north-eastern Delta, possibly Avaris the Hyksos capital. Modern San al-Hagar.
Ta-Kens	Ancient Egyptian meaning Land of the Bow.
Ta-Mery	Ancient Egyptian meaning Black Land.
Taweret	Hippopotamus goddess, protectress of women in labour.
Tefnut	Primeval goddess personifying moisture.
Thoth	Moon god, vizier of the gods, shown as an ibis-headed man.
United with Eternity	The dead form of Amun.
Uraeus	The cobra worn on the king's forehead.
Vizier	Chief minister of an oriental ruler.
Wawet	Northern Nubia.
Winged Disc	See Horus the Behedite.

INDEX